PREPOSTEROUS TALES

First published in 2005 by Sam & Neil
1 Heath Gardens, Twickenham, Middlesex, TW1 4LY

Sam Neil

2 0 0 5

ISBN 1904207375

Printed and bound in China

CONTENTS

INTRO

Wherever there is rock or ice there is potential. A jumble of granite boulders lies chalkless and undiscovered in the vast open plains of Mongolia; the only evidence of human activity is some ancient tribal carvings. In the Canadian Rocky Mountains, an icicle drips in a shady couloir high above the Icefields Parkway. This tiny fragile stalactite will soon become a mighty column, capable of supporting the weight of a human, but only just. A faint, embryonic pulse is always simmering in the wild places of the globe, waiting to be amplified into the beating energy of a climbing experience.

We've poured over maps and journeyed far and wide to look for these moments, and this climbing travelogue is simply an attempt to capture the spirit of our search. We've climbed and travelled with some great people and have seen things which have left us with a sense of humility and reverence. There's so much we'd love to tell you about but we just can't fit it all in. A week of continuous ranting wouldn't do justice to all the tales. So instead, we've selected the diary scribbles and images that give the best retrospective view of the climbs and the countries during an intense four year period of our lives. To us, the climbing lifestyle is timeless and it still provides us with the same scorching sense of being alive that it did from day one. The trick is never to stagnate and to keep raising your game, wherever it takes you. We hope to see you there.

Neil & Tim

HILL HOUSE, NR. ABI
FRILFORD HEATH 390

Dear Mr & Mrs Emmett,

Timothy - Final Place 10/15 63%

Timothy has made a good start. He is a dear little boy, but full of mischief. I have not found that he is wilful or rude, but just up to every prank that is going. His contrite face when caught out is an absolute picture and a good photographer could win a prize were he able to capture Timothy's expression.

He works hard in class, he obviously has a reasonable memory and as he matures I see him managing his lessons with growing ease. He enjoys an enormous range of activities and he has made a valuable contribution to the Greeks by appearing in the good work list 7 times, and scoring over good marks.

Yours sincerely,

Neil

I've always struggled a bit with climbing. Not doing it - of course I can climb any route I choose as soon as I flick out the lights and start to dream - but why I do it. Climbing can be junk food, a gourmet meal or it can be medicine. Usually it's just plain fun, but sometimes it's escapism, in the past providing me with a bleak reminder that I was running away from something. It's ironic that movement on rock can help you make peace with your life and yet one wrong move might take it away. Disillusioned by the sterile comforts of modern existence, the young climber goes out to take a reality bath and satisfy a thirst for context and depth. But the moment of clarity that follows an ascent never lasts. The harder you clutch on to it, the quicker it fades, leaving you with those same feelings of dissatisfaction, and tempting you to go in deeper next time in search of enlightenment. And so the cycle of this false prophecy continues.

Yet as much joy and fulfilment as climbing has brought me, I have finally realised that it's not going to solve any of life's mysteries! And if I spend the rest of my days with all my hopes pinned on those fleeting moments of magic, then I'll miss all the other ones that occur under my nose on a daily basis. The routes are no more important than the stuff that goes on before and after. Climbing has taught me that it's possible to achieve almost anything if you are sufficiently passionate, but it's equally important not to take it all too seriously. The answer lies not in climbing, but in what you can make of the entire experience. The beauty is that it's slightly different for everyone. This is our version of events. Good luck with yours.

THING AC CORDING TO ...

Tim

Our lives revolve around rules and regulations - traffic lights, speed limits, seat belts, time keeping, politics, police, laws, insurance; the list is endless. Conform to society, because you have to! But climbing gives you the chance to break free and create your own path. How hard do you push it, how much gear do you place and in what style? It's all down to you. With so many different styles, modern day climbing offers more choices than ever before. Like chords on a piano, you can find your note, stick with it or move onto another. Variety provides a wealth of opportunity, like a hit of pure oxygen or life with fresh legs. It's easy to be afraid when we are bombarded with uncertainty or the possibility of the unknown. But embrace it and let your judgment guide you through. You'll never find out what's out there unless you check it out! It's your choice whether you steer a path of positive or negative resistance and then manifest the opportunities that are available. So follow your heart, feel the force, believe in your strengths and work on your weaknesses. Be inspired and search out whatever it is that you're looking for. Have fun and enjoy the freedom. Or as Friedrich Nietzsche said:

'I will have it!'

The aim of this book is to capture the spirit of an intensive period of our lives between 1999 and 2003, during which we exported some of the tricks we learnt whilst climbing at home to some more remote regions of the world.

It was the spate of tagging each other as we put up new routes and repeated each other's in the mid 90s, mainly in North Wales, that inspired us to venture further afield. This was one of those periods that older climbers usually reminisce about, where the sun always seemed to shine, your friends were always at the crag and every route was a blinder. It was fuelled by buckets of enthusiasm, a little friendly competition and a fair share of nervousness and doubt. But it was a sharing experience that fitted in perfectly with the stages we had reached in our climbing. We had both become disillusioned with the repetitiveness of sport climbing and so we rejected it in favour of climbing traditional routes onsight, and also using the new-wave British style that is now call 'head-pointing'. This is where a naturally protected climb that is way beyond your onsight capability is practised first on a top rope, providing an exciting fusion of both sport and trad techniques.

CATALYS

During this same period, our frustrations with the fickle winter conditions in Scotland led us into some unorthodox ice axe wielding antics on the crumbling chalk cliffs of southern England. Chalk is an established medium in the UK for practising winter climbing techniques, but we developed a new style using pre-placed ice screw protection, which enabled us to climb much steeper lines than had been possible with previous methods. All this upsidedown action gave us the misguided notion that we should enter the Ice World Cup and get involved in some of the new sport-style mixed climbing that was being practised on the continent.

This era of experimentation had its fair share of scrapes and near misses, but we learnt a great deal from each other's approach. One of us (Tim) was slightly too reckless when we started climbing together and the other needed to realise that sometimes it's actually safer to let go. This whole process laid the foundations for the journey which was to follow by broadening our horizons and exposing us to a wide variety of climbing styles. There is a tendency to want to impose your ethical prejudices when visiting new countries, but you don't want to eat burger and chips in a Vietnamese cafe, or hear Western dance music in a Mongolian night club. When you're so far away from home, why not try something new? There are a hundred and one ways to approach climbing a piece of rock, whether it's ground-up bolting in Cuba or onsight deep water soloing in Majorca. If an ethical style has already been developed in a country, it seems respectful to continue the trend. If, however, you are starting with an empty canvas, then the sky is the limit. Our mission has always been to maximise the amount of adventure and minimise damage to the rock. You need to consider practicalities, but above all else you must search for a style that best enhances the feeling of moving on that particular type of rock.

Tim on Nightmayer, E8 6c, Llanberis, UK, 2nd asc RW
Neil on Gravediggers, E8 6c, Llanberis, UK, 1st asc RW

Neil on Massive Attack, C7,
Saltdean, UK, 1st asc RW
Tim on Demolition Man, C7,
Saltdean, UK, 1st asc CP

It all started in Llanberis in the summer of 95 when I heard a rumour that a lad who the locals referred to as 'strong Tim' had been eyeing up my car.

Not that it was really mine, but I was proud of the fact that I'd blagged it for a part time sales rep job from the climbing manufacturer I was working for. And not that 'strong Tim' had wrongful intentions towards it – apparently, it was just that his banger had broken down in the space behind it and he declared that he'd be driving something like it in years to come. Being from Sheffield, I felt I should reserve judgment for anyone whose name was prefixed with the word 'strong', but I had to admit that I was becoming intrigued with the reputation of this rising local star. Especially when I heard that he was the only man to have avoided hospitalisation or death after a night on the Tequila with old Lee McGinley, and that his girlfriend, in the wake of this achievement, had nicknamed him 'nice but dim!'

> 'When I was informed that Tim Emmett would be 'mad for it', I had no idea just how much this fact would re-shape the next decade of my life.'

Our worlds finally collided a few months later. On a frosty February morning, I drove down the Llanberis Pass on my way to the office to realise in horror that Central Icefall Direct (the route that every ice climber wants to do but can't because it never forms) was in perfect condition. I was chained to the office by day, but rang the local climbing shop to see if anyone would be prepared to have a go at it at night. I popped the question to the guy who answered the phone and when I was informed that Tim Emmett would be 'mad for it', I had no idea just how much this fact would re-shape the next decade of my life.

If we had broken down during the drive up the Pass that night in search of our prize, I felt confident that Tim would have carried both me and the car to our destination. When I released the central locking, he flew out of the car like a greyhound on the starting gun. I threw on my sack and trotted after him into the darkness, but to our dismay, a tiny beam of light began flickering up in the

'Sorry, I was so mad for it, I think I might've moved both axes at the same time!'

distance. Surely it can't be? Our enthusiasm was quickly converted to frustration as we realised we'd been pipped at the post, but we carried on to the base just in case. We watched and sulked as the leader clipped into his axes to take a rest, less than six feet off the ground. Tim let out a large sigh. My suggestion of abandoning ship was met with silence by Tim, who now appeared to be on the verge of spontaneously combusting. He sat down and then immediately stood up again. 'Right, this is what we're going to do - you're going to climb to the left of him as fast as you can and not place any runners. Let's have it!'

It was said with such vigour that I felt compelled to run with the plan and within minutes, I found myself panting for breath with the hot aches on the first belay ledge. I swear that Tim was standing next to me before I had time to put him on belay and before I knew it, he was leading through and up onto the crux wall. The chap below arrived next to me, looking a little phased and slightly disgruntled, as Tim disappeared up into the night above us. 'Your friend's a bit eager', he said. 'I'm sorry, mate - I think he just gets a bit carried awa....' Mid-sentence, the torch beam above us came clattering rapidly downwards and Tim landed perfectly next to us on the ledge with a thud. 'Sorry, I was so mad for it, I think I might've moved both axes at the same time!'

Without stopping to regroup, he was up and at it to finish the job, and soon it was my turn again. I had never climbed a free-standing ice pillar before and the top pitch shone above me in the moonlight like a giant version of Darth Vader's light saber. As I cowered below it, I recalled how it had collapsed on the last person who attempted the climb several years ago - 'But that was because he'd put gear in it!' Tim said. In spite of his optimism, I was all too conscious of our friends down below. Above me and below me was more vertical ice than I was capable of illuminating and yet the usual feelings of exposure were notably absent. We felt like characters in some weird play, and the final assault on the pillar unfolded like an abstract dream sequence. We topped out in a whirl of elation and charged off down the hillside in search of the nearest night club.

It was just past midnight when we arrived in the melting pot of Welsh clubland, Bangor's Octagon Centre. As we screeched into the deserted, windswept car park, kebab wrappers blew around in the amber light and it started to drizzle. Tim bounded up to the old man who was boarding up his fast food stand. 'Scuse me mate - any action going on round here now?' I stopped taking off my salopettes and got back into the car.

The next morning I drove down the pass on my way to work, eager to admire the previous night's handywork; but Central Icefall was gone. And its collapse triggered a chain reaction of climbing, travelling and general mayhem with my new friend which, to this date, is still gathering momentum.

View from Snowdon summit NG
Neil on Central Icefall Direct, VI, pitch 3 TE
Crag y Rhaedr by day with the lines of
Central icefall direct, VI, on the left and
climbers on Cascade, V, on the right NG

'Building character is like building a dam. You should be very careful in making the bank. If you try to do it all at once, water will leak from it.'

Shunryu Suzuki

It was the phase in my life when everything seemed to have gone wrong - I had lost my girlfriend in a climbing accident and my elbows were racked with tendonitis. So I fled the Sheffield sport climbing scene that had been my home and took up residence in North Wales. One day, whilst working in a climbing shop, I bumped into trad guru, Nick Dixon who floored me with a proposal that we should try to repeat Johnny Dawes' mythical Cloggy route, the Indian Face. I laughed at first, but Nick's idea grew into a monster that catapulted me headlong into a whole new world. My quest to repeat the Indian Face became an all-out attempt to re-establish my motives in climbing and set my life straight. And I still shudder today to think just how far out of my depth I became.

'Truth and reality must be embraced fully, in all their dreadful horror and beauty, if the spirit is to live and grow. There must be no fear of the shadows - and we can only understand them if we enter deep into them.'

John Redhead

Neil with Johnny Dawes & Nick Dixon below Cloggy MG
Neil making a top rope attempt at Indian Face E9 6c, Cloggy, UK MG

SLAYING THE BEAST (Neil)

Call it a spell, mystical and enchanting, or call it a curse, but the test here is the ability to say no, to walk away and put out the fire. The walk to Cloggy has now become a necessity to satisfy a drug-like urge.

Each stony step increases the accumulating voltage by a tiny increment and the end product is a belly full of nerves by the time I reach the foot of Great Wall. But today is different, light relief from the usual anguish because I suspect the top's wet. A practising day and for once, a chance to relax and soak up the surroundings. For the first time I don't even bother to look up. Dump my sack, quick drink and turn round in my own time to realise in horror that it's dry.

Wires tripped, I'm thrown into a flurry of automated activity. The routine gear racking and uncoiling of ropes is therapy in the escalating tension. No questioning the moment - this crag is different, so rarely extending the privilege and I know I must rise to the gesture. The usual four hours of psyching must now be squeezed into twenty minutes; no build-up and it's hit me like a steam train. This is the day, and in half an hour I will be free. I'm in so deep now that all I want is an outcome. Deep breaths to clear my head and I'm insignificant compared to the beast which rears up behind me.

We scramble up to the base for the 'belayer's brief': 'Obviously I won't be falling off but...' I position Airlie Anderson at the top of the slope at the base of the wall. Her face says it all, and her timid chuckle as I stumble carelessly on some wet grass does little to diffuse the situation. OK, boots now, this'll be fun. Where has this petty concern for their lacing suddenly come from? I'm not tuning a bloody piano here, yet each tug seems to tighten the knot in my stomach. Rope next, lifeline, umbilical to mother earth, I ponder the irony as my fingers again perform our common task.

How long to sustain this ritual of procrastination? What can I do next? Chalk, that's it, more chalk. Forget it, go now, the groundwork is done. Stooping for one last check that my soles are clean feels like a bow of courtesy. For God's sake, stop this superstition. How can I possibly show any more respect? Eyes closed now, deep breath, touch rock. The beast stirs and the black gargoyle on the skyline laughs and cracks his whip as I step up into the arena. The game begins.

History has made me all too aware of this wall's trickery, so the comparative ease of this first section only serves to unnerve me further. I dither with the choice between two huge spiky jugs and try to ignore the extravagance of such a decision. No time to waste and I'm moving up into line now, yellow brick road, red carpet or just 'the shaft', soaring and tubing towards the sky. I don't notice this next bit and I'm already at the stopper placement at forty feet. 'Stopper' - I love that word and so too must have Redhead, cartwheeling and tumbling from the upper reaches. Best forgotten. Press on and it's actually starting to feel like climbing now, almost relaxing, technically absorbing. A tiny offset nut placement reminds me of Moffatt's escape right. Historic, brave, but eliminate; more a master of route finding.

Kick in now, concentrate. The need to re-chalk my left hand for a tiny nubbin gives me a small reminder of what's to come. The holds are getting smaller now and I mistakenly look down to the stopper. Remind myself that I'm still in range and thank the Lord for sticky rubber as I smear up onto Redhead's tormented moves. Calm down, take stock and clip into the RPs; networks of insecurity. Tiny pieces of brass lodged in the surface veins of this creature's skin. They're gonna hold as far as I'm concerned now. No room for any doubt up here. A dip and I hurriedly swing out right, away from the last gear placement before I allow the significance of the manoeuvre to register. The gargoyle turns to the beast with a knowing sneer as I move past my previous highpoint. From here on the mechanics will be blissfully simple.

To my left are the scars of previous battles. Aroused and angered, the beast sheds its skin in the winter and now the flake is gone. A trivial blemish is left, yet with dire consequences to any challenger. No longer that peg to go for, and as I undercut rightwards, I see Dixon, manic eyes of fire, his words ringing hollow in the back of my head: 'There are no more islands of retreat, you'll just have to go'.

Macabre indeed to fall whilst moving onto the rest ledge but a sudden stab hits me as I realise in disgust that I can't lean back enough to see the crucial foot pocket which is my stepping-stone to temporary sanctuary. Who is doing this? Why does it all feel so different? Behold the transformation of my top-roping companion into a devilish stranger. Dawes spoke of the sparks, no rules to this game, just transient fields of energy - an infinite number of tempting solutions yet an infinite number of blind alleys leading to disaster. Forced to bodge the foot placement, I feel it creeping and just make it onto the ledge before it pops. I'm standing there now, clawing at crystals, torso pressed against the cold rock. My heartbeat pulsing like war drums almost feels strong enough to tip me off backwards and my attempts to slow it down so far have been futile.

This rest ledge is perhaps the beast's greatest irony. Perched on the brink of its gaping jaws, I must now stop and 'rest'. Rest when I'm not even tired. Rest when I'm desperate not to break the continuity of the climbing. Rest and allow my fragile bubble of focus to be burst and the true horror of my position to come flooding in and sweep me away. Come on now, 'be positive', Smythe would say. You can't fall off a 7b+ that you've got wired. For God's sake, it's a formality. Isn't it? For Christ's sake, I just don't know any more.

A faint burning cramp in my calves and I shuffle to try and get some weight on my heels. The rope falling off down to my left, pulling me awkwardly, is perhaps its breath, affecting my balance and stopping me trusting. Then Adam Wainwright's words: 'A rope's just tricking you into being there - you'd be better off solo.' Yet the glimmer of hope it offers me is the only thing I've got to cling to. Somehow this, the second delaying ritual of the day, doesn't frustrate me so much. It's beckoning me now but this time there'll be no going back. The chalked line of crystals above me is my one way ticket to judgment. And the worst thing about this is that it's not even going to call me. I must make the decision to go myself. I consciously force my mind not to wander to the option of rescue for a second. I know from Johnny's experience that I'll only return, so it may as well be now. I'm fully aware that leaving this spot is utterly unjustifiable using any form of logic, but my immense urge to get this over with ought to be enough. I breathe in to announce to Airlie, far down below, that I'm going for it but the thought of how the words will sound prevents me and no sound seems to come out. There is no logical time to do this, so without thought I simply use the obvious progression of the holds to lead me. This is it now, I'm stepping out.

Teetering across the lip of the overlap, the foot change I dread passes with discerning ease. I carefully use my vision's depth-of-field facility to focus only on the intricacies of the smears and not the void below upon which they rest. For a foolish second, I kid myself it's going well. But now comes the move - there had to be one somewhere. My chalk line out left marks the huge but hidden foot pocket which I must step across to, and I'm palpably aware that the urge to perform this move in control will also be the very urge that will cause me to miss it and continue my downward arc. I grip tightly and my right leg starts to shake. Must loosen and allow

'I'm in so deep now that all I want is an outcome.'

The Indian Face E9 6c
RW

The east buttress of Clogwyn d'ur Arddu, with climbers on the classic E3, Great Wall. Indian Face takes a faint line of weakness to the right which becomes increasingly thin and serious with height. This route typifies everything that is unique and thrilling about British traditional climbing. It lures you, then abandons you, and the climax of this 150ft journey is a 40ft run-out through the hardest climbing above an RP2 which provides the only protection between you and the ground. The epic history of its first ascent reads like a Trojan War story - both Crewe and Fowler made early scrapings but it was John Redhead who was left a broken man after his siege culminated in a 70ft ground-scraping tumble. He placed a bolt and vowed to return, but instead abandoned the line. Jerry Moffatt chopped the bolt and tried to settle the score but instead found an escape route rightwards avoiding the main challenge. It took the vision of Johnny Dawes to lay things to rest and his long awaited ascent in 1986 set the climbing world alight. But the saga continued. Whilst playing on an abseil rope a year later, Redhead dislodged a hollow flake which housed the tiny knife-blade peg which 'protected' the crux on Dawes's ascent - an act which deterred future ascentionists further still. Today, this awe inspiring route is still regarded as one of the great challenges of British climbing.

THE INDIA

myself to go. I shut my eyes and fall across kicking violently to seat my foot. I stop in balance but for a second my mind continues churning downwards and I feel nauseous.

120 feet and with four hard moves to go, the RP is now too low to save me anyway and I can't take a hand off to dip. A brittle side-pull bites into my sweaty and unchalked fingertips causing them to creep. Stepping high onto a sloping boss, I drive upwards, the tension in my thigh causing me to shake further. Both legs shaking now and as I extend with the key for Dawes' crucial three-finger crystal cluster for my right, I realise for the first time what this thing is doing to me. As if spreading like a cancer, this tremor is now in my forearms and hands too. I'm unable to arrange my fingers just so and I'm not sure whether I dare move from here. Facing the hardest move in the sequence I'm staring headlong into its eyes. How can this be happening - a full body shake beyond my control? Like a trivial fly, it is trying to shed me. Moves I once knew intimately are now to be onsighted by a strange vibrating body which is slowly being torn apart by its

FACE

mind. Creeping hands on borrowed time, I race to move my feet. This precariously high step-up is at the limit of my flexibility at the best of times, but now, as I try to lift my rigor-mortised leg, I realise that I can't lean back enough to make room for it. I can't even see the foot spike and now desperate, I realise that scraping my face against the rock is the only way to stay on. Stop breathing, heart burning, like raising my own guillotine, the more I lift my leg, the more it throws me off backwards; and yet I must lift it. As I drive up, I feel myself melting into a timeless vacuum. For a split second of complete tranquility, I actually don't mind giving in and resign myself to the unimaginable. But wait. My foot hits the spike and I sway, realising that I'm still on. As if mocking me and with the last hard move still to go, the bastard's given me another chance. Almost laughing as I flail up desperately, left foot well seated now, I duck my head to one side and lash out for the undercut in front of my face. Balance. The tremor subsides like a banished curse. Finishing jug looms and I hurriedly build my feet on smears, hand straining on the flake. Extending now, like reaching out for the grail, knife poised for the

kill. I stretch, plunging, fingers curl, sink and lock. The beast roars and the deep tremors within the mountain are not enough to shake me off now. Sixty feet out from the forgotten RP, clipping the bomber nut which protects the easy upper groove and I'm sliding my sword back into its scabbard. The sun has come out to soak the rock above me like spilt blood and I am released. Darkness of the void beneath, the beast is dying and I'm pulling out into the light.

Cwm d'ur Arddu is warm and still as I melt back into the grassy sanctuary of the belay ledge. Shimmering lake and strolling clouds. Senses unmasked, I realise for the first time that the creature I've slaughtered lived not within these cathedral-like walls but in the walls of my own skull. Trudging off down the path, glowing all over, the scree makes a hollow echo beneath my feet, piercing the quietness. My floating mind wanders to the great unclimbed line on the wall high up left from the pinnacle and suddenly I feel a strange, sickening stirring inside me. I turn round with a start to reassure myself that, of course, there is nothing there.

HOMELA GR LA

'True movement is born
from stillness.'

ITSTONE
NDS

**Master's Edge,
E7 6b, Millstone**
Neil, Ground-up ascent NG

When Ron Fawcett snatched the last great unclimbed arête at Millstone in 1983, it was hailed as the work of a master. The route looked about as climbable as the side of the average house and the only protection was to be found in the quarried shot holes which are located tantalisingly at half height. Rumour had it that if the belayer reacted quickly enough and ran back, they might be able to save the leader from a fall from the last move. Whilst making your blood run cold, it's always the tales like this that get under your skin. There is nothing to match the sense of occasion that comes with arriving at the base of a route that you'd dreamt about for years and hoping that you're finally ready.

THE BLACK ROCKS SAGA (Tim)

Setting up for the last move on End of the Affair, the infamous E8 arete at Curbar, I realised something was wrong. I shouted down to Neil who was belaying:
'Err... I'm not up for it!'
'What!' he replied, horrified.
'You can't say that... You've got no choice!'

Neil was poised, ready to jump off the ledge that lies below, so he could take in enough rope to prevent a ground fall. Instinctively and very carefully, I started reversing. I knew if I could get closer to the gear, and Neil jumped, I would probably stop just short of the ground. Seconds later, I was off. Neil leapt from the ledge and we came to a halt hanging like a couple of monkeys at a fairground stall, just a few inches from the ground. Words didn't really seem sufficient at the time but I had to say something: 'That was a bit spicy! Nice one!'

A week later we hatched a cunning plan to go to Curbar in the morning so I could finish End of the Affair and then go on to Black Rocks so Neil could make the second ascent of Meshuga. Then we'd both do Gaia afterwards. Right then! Monday morning started like a dream with crisp blue skies and frozen puddles on the ground. End of the Affair passed without incident this time, and we set off to Black Rocks. A sinister and macabre place at the best of times, I stood beneath the prow of Meshuga while Neil tightened his flimsy shoelaces, preparing to embark on this 'ultimate hard grit experience'. The characteristic signs of anxiety were starting to invade and Neil was silent in his meditative void. He started the dynamic sequence of moves with the rope dangling uselessly to the redundant belay plate that I clutched in my sweaty palms. I thought about the bouldering mats that he had stashed purposely at the other end of the cliff to prevent temptation. This was a route, not a boulder problem. He'd also made the tough call not to wear a helmet through fear that it would restrict his movement. Maybe our pride and prejudices tread the fine line between self-preservation and recklessness.

**End of the Affair,
E8 6c, Curbar**
Neil RW

Gritstone's pioneers have conjured up some bizarre and optimistic rope systems in their quests to protect the unprotectable, and Johnny Dawes pushed things to a new level with his 1986 Curbar creation, End of the Affair. The only runner on this airy and compelling arête is placed from a boulder at the base of the route before the climbing even starts! A sequence of increasingly on-off moves leads to a final crux reach for a sloping ramp, at which point the runner is barely at a third height! But Dawes reckoned the belayer could throw themselves off a cliff below the route and that there might still be a chance! The route's reputation was further enhanced by the curse which fell upon the belayers. After belaying Dawes on the first ascent, Nick Dixon came back to make the second ascent belayed by Andy Popp who went onto make the third ascent. Neil's ascent was the first to break the curse and Tim's was one of few to test the protection system!

END OF THE AFFAIR

MESHUGA

**Meshuga, E9 6c,
Black Rocks**
Neil, 2nd ascent RW

Anyone who has seen
the video 'Hard Grit' will
remember the sight of Seb
Grieve slapping wildly up this
unprotected battleship arête
which leans out airily over a
steep boulder-strewn slope.
Seb's sadistic laughter and
demonic chanting during the
ascent confirmed his choice
of route name ('Meshuga' is
Yiddish for insane). A sense
of darkness and foreboding
hangs over this gritstone
monolith, which epitomises
everything about climbing that
makes your stomach churn.

Thirty feet up, Neil launched for the blind slap around the arête, hit the sloper, then, like a piece of al dente spaghetti hanging from a kitchen ceiling, he paused, before plummeting down onto the slab just to my left. He bounced off the boulders and down into the gully below. Mike Robertson dropped his camera and legged it down to him while I frantically untied myself from the belay. Dazed and confused, Neil had received a blow to the head. He was incoherent, but there was no blood. After a few moments to recuperate, we took him down to the car and sped off to the hospital. He had been extremely lucky; or so we thought.

A few weeks later the perversion had set in again and we were back at Black Rocks. Our plans to do Gaia had been curtailed for obvious reasons; but I was keen to settle the score. The impact of the Meshuga fall had left Neil suffering from bouts of dizziness whenever he moved his head quickly. Added to that he was a bit spun out to be back at Black Rocks, but was keen to belay. As I reached for the last hold, Neil looked up to me and then down to check the rope. Suddenly he started to spin out and in his mystified state, was convinced I had fallen off. But were his eyes deceiving him? The implications of this decision were critical: if I had fallen, he must run back to take in rope and prevent me from hitting the ground. If I was still climbing and he ran with the rope, then he'd pull me off and impale me on the prow or even the ground. He hung in there, but only just. After topping out, stoked by the ascent, I untied and scooted down the gully to share success with my friend, only to find him crumpled up in a ball with his head in his hands, completely distraught from the ordeal.

The walk to the crag from the Black Rocks car park was becoming a pilgrimage and a year later, I found myself completing it once again. Neil had recovered by this stage and returned to make a successful ascent of Meshuga. But this time, it was my turn to tie into the sharp end, with Charlie Woodburn belaying. No matter how many times I practised, it always felt at my limit. As I stood there contemplating whether today was the day, I couldn't help thinking about Neil's fall. What had changed so much when he tried to lead it - causing him to blow it? Would it happen to me too? I knew Neil had found the climbing easier than I. There was no way that I could climb it eight times in a row on a top rope. My mind raced as the adrenaline floodgates burst open once again. It was now or never.

The first moves passed in a blur and I set up for the infamous knee move that I'd been dreading. I started my sequence: shut your eyes, push, push with your left leg, fully extended, lock as far as you can with your left arm, and then a bit more, reach as far as you can with your right and walk your fingers up into the sloping dish. Open your eyes. I had it. Nothing could prepare me for the overwhelming release when I finally reached the protection at forty feet. Everything went into meltdown but in the distant haze I remember hearing Charlie's jovial voice beckoning me upwards. Staying there for several minutes, I had a few words with myself to calm down before setting off to join the vision of a jubilant Seb Grieve topping out on his first ascent; an image that will stay in my mind forever.

'He bounced off the boulders and down into the gully below.'

Tim on Meshuga,
E9 6c, Black Rocks CW
Frost leaf IP

Gaia, E8 6c, Black Rocks
Neil RW

Immortalised by the film 'Stone Monkey', Johnny Dawes deemed his Black Rocks masterpiece to be too serious to lead again for the camera, but the sight of him top-roping it was enough. An excruciating move seemed to bar access to a compelling groove which later blanked out just at the point where the protection seemed too low to help. To exit from here, Dawes made a nail biting sloping traverse rightwards and a final launch for the arête, all which seemed about as unjustifiable as could be imagined. Ten years on in the film 'Hard Grit', visiting Frenchman Jean Minh Trin Thieu escaped by the skin of his teeth with only a gashed shin to show for his mistake. The Gaia hypothesis, which explores the fusion of man with nature, states that if we listen to the planet we will survive but if we use force we will be the authors of our own demise..

GAIA

'As I flow through the moves, I am only partially aware of what I am doing.'

Chalk hand prints IP

**Harder Faster,
E9 6c, Black Rocks**
Charlie Woodburn, 1st ascent NG

The much-eyed direct finish
to Gaia. It seems ludicrous
to talk of Dawes' original line
as an escape route, but the
continuation straight up the
arête is even more technical
and serious than the sister
route. The extension offers
no additional protection and
culminates in a sloping traverse
along the top of the block
which finishes with one of those
mantelshelves where you have
to scrape everything against
the wall in order to stay on!
The move pictured is one of the
hardest in the sequence and
a fall from here might just be
salvageable. But from then on,
you're on your own..

HARDER FASTER

HARDER FASTER (Neil)

It's a disturbing feeling when a
trusted friend turns out to be psychotic.
And to think that Charlie Woodburn
had been displaying all the signs whilst
staying in our house in Sheffield when
he was trying his project – the direct
finish to Gaia at Black Rocks.

We'd noticed his insomnia, the mood swings and his
slow withdrawal from society, but it didn't register
until it was too late. When Tim and I eventually tried
Harder Faster ourselves on a top rope after Charlie
had made his successful lead, we came away with
a feeling that a friend of ours had done something
really, really bad. As the relatives always say with
hindsight, 'If only we'd realised, we'd have tried to talk
him out of it, or at least called the police.'

HARDER FASTER (Charlie)

'As I flow through the moves I am only partially
aware of what I am doing. My thoughts are hazy, in a
self-induced state of obedience. The body leads and
the mind follows, always one step behind, always in
a state of humble acknowledgement, registering the
present as it flows, unaware of the future or past,
free from the savage responsibility of thought. Fear
and thought are synonymous and consequently the
most frightening part of the ascent coincides with the
only moment of dominance my mind has: the decision
to go. Concentration is of the essence, the act of
stupefying the senses and allowing myself to follow
the drift of my own body. As I climb, I feel as though
I am leaving myself behind, and by giving myself up
to the moment of the rock, by concentrating myself
into the subtle tensions the moves require, I am able
to escape the obligation to think, and this more than
anything else brings me a measure of peace.'

Grit moor and sign MR
Green and yellow ferns IP

'Whether or not it is possible is not the point. If it is our inmost desire to get rid of our self-centred ideas, we have to do it. Before you determine to do it there is difficulty, but once you start to do it, you have none. Your effort appeases your inmost desire. There is no other way to attain calmness.'

Shunryu Suzuki

TRAINING TIPS (Neil)

You can never conquer a piece of rock but it may let you climb it if you are first prepared to yield. It knows not of you and your fragile mortality, but is quietly telling you to move. So shut up and listen so that you can hear with full clarity at the beckoning moment. Don't be aggressive or scared, just be ready. Use its inanimate nature to neutralise your emotions and its random form to direct your flow. Give yourself readily to the flames without holding back the tiniest trace. True movement is born from stillness, and it is only when you allow yourself to be truly released that pure climbing can take place.

**Equilibrium,
E10 7a, Burbage**
Neil, 2nd ascent MR

How long can you continue pushing purely for the sake of it? When a route has truly taken everything you can give and you've walked away to tell the tale, then it seems logical to quit while you're ahead. As such, my repeat of Neil Bentley's Burbage route Equilibrium marked that point. No other route has demanded such specific preparation: special yoga exercises were devised, replica boulder problems were trained on, attempts were abandoned over a few degrees in temperature or a fingertip that was too thin. It was like doing my hardest sport and trad route in the same piece of climbing. Ben Moon originally gave the route French 8b+ as a top rope problem and it was clear that a prospective leader could only get away with falling from the first half of the sequence. After taking nine ground-sweeping falls from just below the red line, I was on my knees, but on the last attempt of the day, it decided to give me a chance. When a route like this opens the door, you have no choice but to go through, and the experience leaves you numb for months, if not the rest of your life.

EQUILIBRIUM

HOMELA

'My new lightweight wetsuit was clearly
going to come in handy!'

SEASCLIFF

Tim swimming away from Jaws NG
Treaddur Bay TE
Pembroke archway MR
Neil on Wet T Shirt Contest,
7a+, Pembroke, 1st asc MR
Mrs Weston herself! AKA Ma Weston
of Bosherston café fame MR

**Chicama, E9 6c,
Treaddur Bay**
Tim, 1st ascent RW

Named after my favourite wave,
the longest left-hand point break
in the world, Chicama packs in
about as much climbing as you
could possibly squeeze into a
route of this height. A counter
diagonal to Big George Smith's
route 'Treacherous Underfoot',
it starts with a 25 ft deep water
solo before embarking onto the
impending steepness with only
just enough protection. Snappy
rock, buckets of lactic acid, a
great sense of urgency and a
final leap off the top. A very
entertaining escapade!

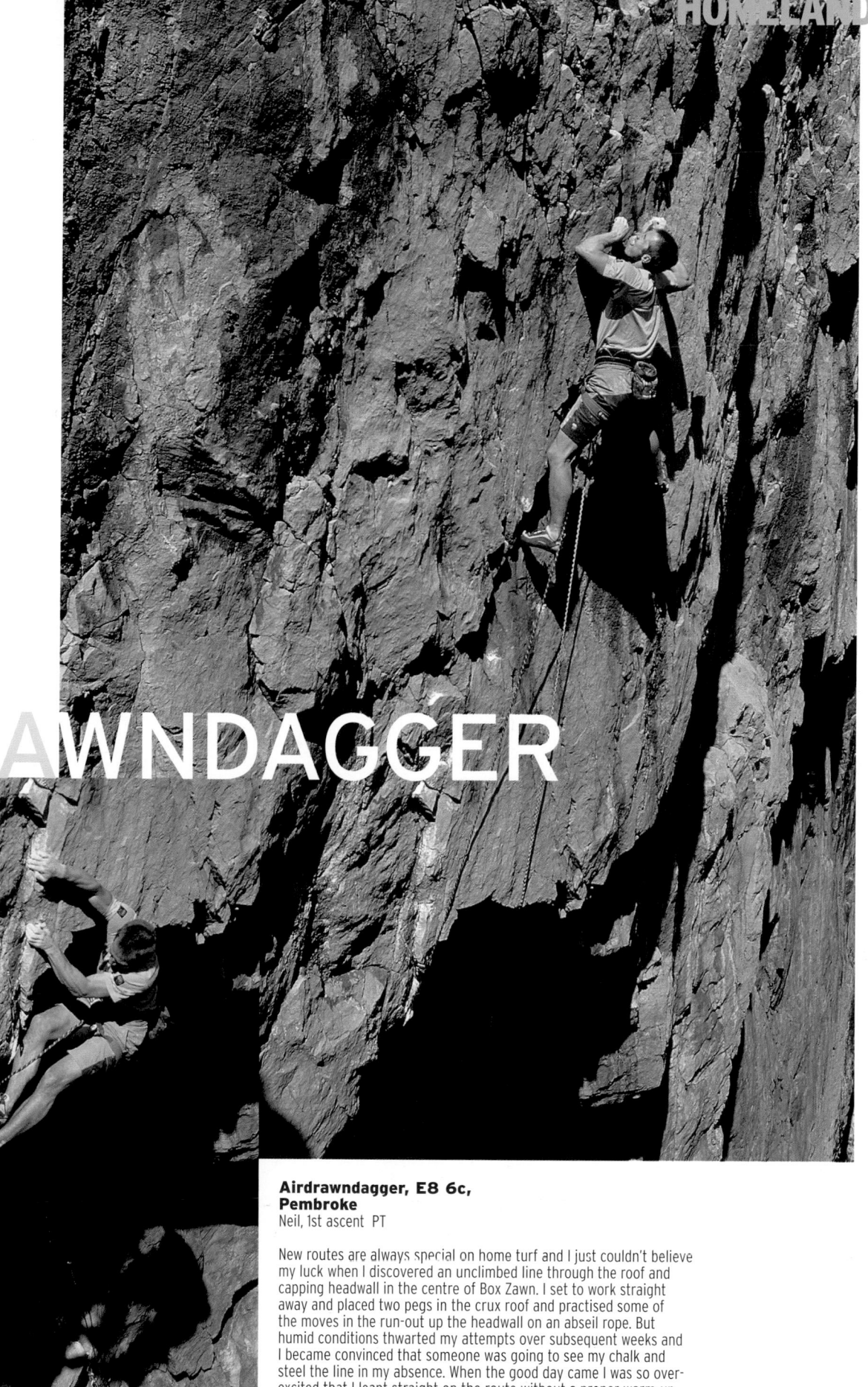

AIRDRAWNDAGGER

Airdrawndagger, E8 6c, Pembroke

Neil, 1st ascent PT

New routes are always special on home turf and I just couldn't believe my luck when I discovered an unclimbed line through the roof and capping headwall in the centre of Box Zawn. I set to work straight away and placed two pegs in the crux roof and practised some of the moves in the run-out up the headwall on an abseil rope. But humid conditions thwarted my attempts over subsequent weeks and I became convinced that someone was going to see my chalk and steel the line in my absence. When the good day came I was so over-excited that I leapt straight on the route without a proper warm-up. The subsequent burn-out caused me to take the biggest fall of my life from the very last move and with the finishing jug in my hand! Surfers always down-play the height of waves but climbers are the opposite when describing their falls – a 15 footer soon becomes 30 ft with a pint of beer in your hand; but this was a definite 50 footer and I actually heard a whooshing noise as I cut through the air! The final ascent was made in the nick of time after a long rest, just as the tide came in and submerged Tim's belay ledge.

'Forget everything they told you at climbing school... It's time to go Deep Water Soloing!'

THE SAFETY WET (Neil)

With new eyes, fresh possibilities can sometimes appear on your doorstep.

The limestone sea cliffs of Pembrokeshire in South Wales are an established home for epic tales of trad climbing endeavour. If you haven't abseiled into the sea with a full rack of gear or been consumed, mid-belay by the rising tide, then you haven't experienced the full Pembroke wrath.

The obvious problems of access and escape have meant that the cliffs which have been developed tend to be those which offer adequate protection and a ledge to abseil down to. Until recently, the steep blank walls which drop straight into the sea have remained elusive territory. But a radical change of approach has unlocked their potential. Forget everything they told you at climbing school and throw that rack of gear in the sea! Choose a warm day with a calm sea. Bring plenty of pairs of shoes, some like-minded accomplices and a kilo of chalk with you. Scramble down for a swim to check the depth, and you're away. Let others spend hours fiddling in gear and freeing jammed ropes - it's time to go deep water soloing!

**Hunter Killer,
E6 6b/F7b,
Huntsman's Leap**
Tim, onsight solo MR

This trad test piece rises from the gloomy depths of Huntsman leap, and its base is only accessible during a frustratingly brief window at low tide. Add sparse protection to the equation and slowly a different strategy starts to emerge. Reverse the tables, abseil in at high tide and you've got yourself a major deep water solo challenge! Although most of the hard climbing is in the first half of the route, there's a difficult move at 80 feet (pictured) so be sure not to fall off here!

Neil & Tim in the Pembroke drying room MR

HUNT

CR KILLER

**Freeborn Man,
F6c, Swanage**
Leah Crane, onsight solo MR

The crowd goes silent during
the defining moment of the
2002 summer deep water
soloing festival at Swanage
in Dorset. Our pal Leah Crane,
rather like most 13 year olds,
had never soloed before and
the idea of falling in the sea
was, she told us 'worse than
landing on flat ground', seeing
as she'd never swum in it
before. But a day of spectating
from the cliff top took its toll.
After viewing a succession of
epic successes and failures
on Freeborn Man, Leah asked,
'I think I'd like to have a go?'
We rallied round to make sure
that the full safety crew was
in place, but she dispatched it
without incident.

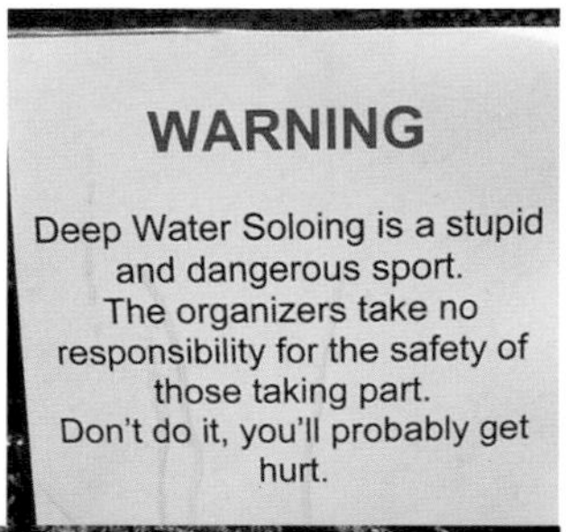

FREEBORN MAN

'The idea of falling in the sea was, she told us 'worse than landing on flat ground.'

Stair Hole, Lulworth MR
Tim on Freeborn Man,
F6c, Swanage IP

Mark of the Beast,
F7c, Lulworth
Tim AH

Originally led with bolt protection
and then soloed by the first
ascencionist Pete Oxley, Mark of
the Beast has to be one of the most
important routes in the history
of deep water soloing. When Leo
Houlding, Neil and I turned up to
attempt it in the summer of 1998,
it had never had a ground-up
solo ascent. The race was on! Not
long after Leo and I were both
dispatched just inches from the top,
I heard the cheers as he topped
out on his second try. I couldn't get
my rock shoes on fast enough. Big
moves between even bigger holds
lead to a few cheeky ones thrown
in at the top just where you least
need them; it couldn't have been
designed better! I just managed to
save enough strength for the last
move crux and made it to the top
and Neil just managed to follow.
This route is so much fun, superb!

Swordfish Trombones,
F7a+, Swanage
Tim AH

This was undoubtedly the first
route to demonstrate the true
benefits of deep water soloing.
Premiere DWS pioneer Crispin
Waddy originally tackled the
line with a rope and full trad
rack but was unable to make
progress through the crux
at the final roof. So instead,
he resorted to soloing it in
order to make the first ascent,
lightweight and unhindered.
Conner cove has now become
the most popular DWS venue in
the UK, and it boasts a range
of classic solos to its name.

SWORDFIS

'Mark of the Beast has to be one
of the most important routes in
the history of deep water soloing.'

TROMBONES

'The steep blank walls which drop straight into the sea have remained elusive territory.'

Jaws, F8a, Pembroke
Tim, 1st ascent MR

If there's one thing I look forward to the most in the British summer, it's the deep water soloing festival. Loads of smiling faces, great climbing and an even better party! All I had to do was finish my project and I would have something to celebrate that night, but so far things hadn't been going to plan. I had been trying the central battleship prow at Broadhaven crag and Neil had cleaned a finish up the hideous crumbling band of rock at 60 feet, so I could attempt it on-sight, ground up. Late in the afternoon and after a string of attempts, I found myself staring the exit holds in the face. It's in the bag! Smash! Suddenly, I flew off backwards and my hold struck me square in the face. No! I took the 50 ft plunge for the 8th time! What more can I possibly do? My arms are torched but I know that if I can only get up it before the party, then it's going to be one of the best nights ever. But Jaws had drawn blood and by now the adrenaline was seriously flowing. I head up a final time, get to my high point, find something, hang it... I'm there, I'm there. I topped out with a beaming smile. Yeah!

JAWS

THE WIZARD

The Wizard, F8a, Pembroke
Neil, ground-up 1st ascent MR

It stood to reason that there had to be new cliffs hidden away somewhere that would be even better for DWS - the question was how to find them. The touch paper was lit one night at a party in North Wales when Crispin Waddy (the godfather of DWS who has scoured every inch of the Pembrokeshire coastline in a sea kayak) decided to retire and hand over his projects! We couldn't get over to Kato Zawn fast enough. The back wall revealed a soaring flake-line that overhung consistently for 45 degrees and looked utterly compelling. But you couldn't get to it on a rope even if you tried. Ground-up solo would be the only way and my new lightweight wetsuit was clearly going to come in handy! Three days of effort and over ten splash-downs later, I found myself pulling over the top. But the Wizard was just the start of the Pembroke DWS Renaissance.

Rick Smee, Mike Robertson
and Seb Grieve in city NG
Rio night skyline MR
Slacklining on Ipanema beach MR
Corcovado above Rio MR

BRAZ
BLA

'We were going to have to remove
all hedonistic distractions.'

ME IT ON RIO

'It seemed appropriate to stop for a second and celebrate the fact that we hadn't been shot.'

CITY OF GOD (Neil)

'Every climber who visits Rio wants to do the Corcovado', Fabiano our host had told us.

After all, who wouldn't want to climb a thousand feet of perfect granite and be greeted at the top by the enormous statue of Christo Redentor, glowing above the city's skyline? 'We usually manage to put them off though!' he added with a chuckle. It transpires that there are only two free routes on this mighty wall anyway. One is a technically amenable but sewage-smeared chimney, whose crux is to negotiate a jammed refrigerator that was hurled into it from the tourist centre above. The other is the unrepeated and reputedly desperate 'Itavo Passagero', which is rumoured to be any grade in excess of 7b+. And those who do manage to choose from this menu are usually put off by the starter course: the forest land below the wall lies next to one of Rio's most notorious favellas, and the gruesome tales of bandit activities are enough to deter anyone from walking to the base unless they carry an uzi as a standard item of climbing equipment.

For these reasons, Rick Smee and I had tried our best to ignore the Corcovado during our first few weeks in Rio, but it just wouldn't go away. Perhaps if we left early there'd be no bandits and surely we could crank this local test piece in a day if the leader freed and the second aided? It wasn't until the last Saturday of our trip that we decided to pack our kit and brace ourselves for the disappointment of an early night in the partying capital of the world. As we paced around the apartment a final time, the phone rang. Fabiano was charged up: 'Hey boys – it's all laid on: supermodel party at Mele Melo's. You guys are on the guest list. Meet first in Ipanema for drinks. Come on let's do it!' Now we all know the look that climbers exchange at moments like this. Neither of us wanted to be the one to break. So we winced with pain and stood firm in our resolve. Sure the supermodels will wait for us, 'Itavo Passagero here we come!'

The alarm went off at 5am and we stumbled out into the streets. As we boarded the number 174 bus which goes through the main part of Rio to the Corcovado, we pondered the novelty of going Big Wall free climbing in a city centre. 'Those bastards will be turning out of Mele Melo's now', said Rick. 'Yeah but we get the route,' I said with a total lack of conviction. The obvious glowing white cross in the sky marked the spot to jump off the bus. A mad head-torch thrash through the forest ensued which deposited us at the bottom of the route just as the sun rose. We'd allowed ourselves to become so psyched out by the idea of bandits that it seemed appropriate to stop for a second and celebrate the fact that we hadn't been shot.

Less than two hours later we found ourselves sitting in exactly the same spot with our tails planted firmly between our legs. Two easy pitches had led to the so-called 'crux' pitch, which as far as I was concerned

RAZURA

Neil on Razura, E4 5c, Rio MR

was virtually impossible. We'd been told to expect something technical but this had been preposterous - a vertical wall that was featureless apart from the tiny crystals which bonded it together and an ominous bolt ladder. My fingertips were completely shredded and I'd made it no higher than the second bolt. 'Definitely conditions', I said. 'I bet they all had rich boyfriends anyway', Rick replied. And to add insult to injury we had to make the forest dash again in peak bandit time.

In spite of making it back down to the road alive, spirits were lower than usual on the number 174 bus back to Urca. We'd become so used to this chaotic journey by now that we sat in a daze, filtering out the surrounding chaos. But then suddenly the bus steered to avoid an area that had been cordoned off with riot tape, and I was jolted back into consciousness. We were ushered to a halt by police and I noticed that a commotion was starting to build. The bus pulled away again and it wasn't until we got home that we were told the news. A young man had boarded the number 174 bus in Botafogo and taken a woman hostage at gunpoint, only hours after Rick and I had made the same journey. The police blundered the affair and shot the woman before eventually shooting the man.

On the 23rd July 1993, one of the bloodiest tragedies in modern Brazilian history took place. In an incident known as the massacre Candelaria, the police opened fire on a group of orphans that were sheltering illegally in a cathedral in the centre of Rio. Eight were killed, but the assailant on the number 174 bus that day was the last of the known survivors. I know I'm so often guilty of using climbing as a smokescreen to hide from the real world, but this was one day when it cleared with a blast.

Boiling Point crag, Itataiai National Park
MR

The zigzag flake left of centre went at E4. Seb Grieve's route Fuzzy Logic, E7 6b, takes the dark streak up the centre. Neil's route Boiling Point, E8 6b, takes the faint pink streak to its right and Mike Robertson's Dogging Chop, E6 6b climbs a shallow groove just right of the obvious overlap.

'For us Brits who would put up seven lines, including a girdle traverse on a crag the size of a public toilet block, it was more than we could cope with.'

BOILING POINT (Neil)

It was all we could do to drag ourselves away from Rio, but if we were going to salvage any credibility for our so-called 'climbing expedition',

we realised that we were going to have to remove all hedonistic distractions. The remote granite moorland area of Itataiai National Park which lies between Rio and Sao Paolo was the chosen venue to steer us back on course. As we trundled out of the city limits and up into the mountains, the motivation that had so nearly deserted us seemed to return in full force. Ralf, our guide - a quiet and solemn character who reminded me of a wise Red Indian chief - had hardly spoken all journey, but a glint was starting to appear in his eye. 'There's a good crag there, there, there, there... and there', he said pointing in a 360 degree radius, 'and all with no routes.' For us Brits who would put up seven lines, including a girdle traverse on a crag the size of a public toilet block, it was more than we could cope with. We pitched camp and hurried off to the crag which looked through the binoculars to be the pick of the bunch.

Neil and Seb Grieve
curb crawling MR
Seb on truck MR
Tent in Itataiai MR

'Nobody wants to do climbs like this; you just want to have done them.'

Seb Grieve and I abseil-inspected two subtle but distinct lines on a beautiful fifty metre high shield of smooth granite. The protection on both routes was virtually non-existent but we'd vowed not to use bolts and the climbing looked so brilliant that we were already completely hooked. After a session of top-rope practice and a night of no sleep, we returned the next morning to face the music. Seb opted for a surprise attack, jumping straight on his route before he had a chance to think better of it. As he attempted to lose himself in the climbing, the usual trademark running commentary of fake laughter and verbal diarrhoea did little to convince any of us far below on the ground that he wasn't in an extremely serious situation. As he disappeared over the top into the meadows with a whoop of joy, the pressure was magnified and planted firmly onto my shoulders. Nobody wants to do climbs like this; you just want to have done them. It then occurred to me, at the worst possible moment, that this was not the same game of delusion that we play back home. No mobile phone call to a helicopter rescue service that would plant you in a fully equipped hospital if things went wrong. I shuddered at the thought of what might happen if... and then quickly forced it out of my head. It was this blocking process that triggered the moment.

But there was something profoundly disturbing about the ascent which followed. On climbs of this length, it is unrealistic to expect to be able to maintain the empty-minded, trance-like state that is essential for the shorter gritstone test pieces back home. The best you can hope for is to keep your conscious mind at bay on the hard sections and to allow it to seep back through on easier ground. When it happens the other way round, you know you're in for a rough ride. At a hundred feet and far above pointless runners, as I entered the crux my foot crept on a smear, which sent a shot of adrenaline straight to the heart. The reaction was to stab my other foot out violently and the reaction to this was for my hips to start swaying outwards from the rock. At this point, I handed everything over to the deranged autopilot of a runaway train, and was whipped up and dumped at the top of the crag. The warm sense of relief as I came round was soon tempered as I pieced it all back together. After all, I had vowed previously that I would never again surrender all semblance of control to the outcome of the dice.

Rick Smee high bouldering, Itataiai MR
Mike Robertson on Dogging Chop, E6
6b, Itataiai, 1st asc NG

Neil on Boiling Point,
E8 6h, Itataia, 1st asc MR

BOILING POINT

CANA
THE GREAT

DAYS WHITE WEST

'The Captain's in-car thermometer had displayed a consistent temperature of below minus thirty.'

Mark Garthwaite and
Calgary graffiti NG
Tyre and snow chains NG
Hand on coffee cup IP
Nightfall over Icefields Parkway NG

SILVER TASSEL

'Any metal you touched tore at your flesh.'

Mark Garthwaite and mad ice features NG
Mark Garthwaite on Silver Tassel, Field Region, WI 4 NG
Frozen lake footprints NG

THE ASYLUM

The Asylum, M7+, Jasper region
Neil MG

Sometimes the best plans are made on the spur of the moment. When Garth and I pulled into the lay-by below our chosen ice target for the day - the French Maid - we were somewhat disgruntled after the long drive and early start to see that it had collapsed in the night. The only other option nearby was Sean Isaac's 5-pitch mixed creation, The Asylum, a route whose top pitch was rumoured to be somewhere on another planet. Three pitches of easy ice led us to a cave from which a ludicrously inaccessible ice dagger was suspended. In spite of the bolts, we couldn't have been more psyched out; but I drew the straw and set-off scratching my way up the bulging yellow rock. As I swung out onto the crucial traverse my fingers started uncurling from my axes, but it wasn't just my arms that were melting in the afternoon sun - each time I kicked out desperately to try and get a bridge rest on the ice, it just broke away. One last attempt before toppling off in exhaustion and at last my crampons bit. I took a few minutes to gather myself before committing to the mind-blowing finale under the curtain and onto the ice wall above.

Icicles from roof NG
Mist around Banff NG

STUCK IN THE GHOST (Neil)

'You boys stick with me' said our host, Captain Keen. 'I'll see you right!'

Garth and I giggled nervously as we bounced around in the back of Glaswegian ex-pat Alan Kerr's 4 wheel drive. Alan, as well as being the keenest ice climber in the world, is also one of those characters who gives you the feeling that the only way he'll know when to stop is when he's gone too far. We were miles away from anywhere in a remote region of the Canadian Rockies called the Ghost, and the stories of climbers getting stuck in their vehicles and freezing to death were fresh in my mind, mainly because the Captain insisted on repeating them. 'Tricky bit coming up', he said, as we started sliding out of control down a firebreak between dense pine forest. The powder was getting deeper and deeper and the Captain's in-car thermometer had displayed a consistent temperature of below minus thirty. 'Bit of momentum required here boys', and the Captain belted it out of the trees towards a large snow drift. The bull bars dipped and I felt that sinking feeling as we lost traction, but the Captain wrestled with the controls and we cleared our obstacle. 'Only the creek to go now lads', whooped our hero. 'We'll be on the route in no time!'

Garth and I exchanged glances as we hurtled towards the river bank, but resistance at this point was futile. As we bounced down onto the icy crust, it heaved and subsided. The Captain gave it full throttle but we ground to a halt. 'Happens all the time guys - we'll be out in a jiffy.' He promptly leapt out of the warm cabin and jumped into the knee-deep icy water, clutching a metal spade with his bare hands. The frantic shovelling performance that followed must be the most impressive feat of pain tolerance that I've ever witnessed – and I was convinced that we would soon have a 4-limb frostbite case on our hands. We begged him to stop but the Captain was on a mission. Garth and I supported by fetching branches to ram under the tyres. But after two hours of effort we were still just as stuck.

'There's only one thing for it', announced Garth after lengthy consideration, 'We're going to have to fell some trees.' I was surprised to hear this from a keen Greenpeace supporter, but the job had to be done, even though I failed to see how a few logs would provide the answer to our plight. Another hour had passed by the time we had managed to carefully position some logs and create a fulcrum system. This was it now, with only a few hours of daylight left, we were down to our last idea. The Captain took up his position in the cockpit while Garth and I braved the water for the first time to man the levers. On the count of three, he floored it and we leant on the logs with all our might. Water sprayed in all directions, drenching me and Garth to the skin, but we dived out of the way to leave room for the beast as it reared up and reversed onto dry land.

'Right then boys', said the Captain, 'let's go climbing!'

THE SORC

'The stories of climbers getting stuck in their vehicles and freezing to death were fresh in my mind.'

The Sorcerer, WI 5+, Ghost region
MG

(Neil) After our episode getting the truck stuck in the creek, Garth and I felt fairly timid about returning to the Ghost region, especially with Captain Keen at the wheel! But we were equally determined to search out this classic four-pitch ice pillar and so agreed on a rematch. This was a day when the powder on the approach was waist deep and the temperatures were so low that any metal you touched tore at your flesh. We stumbled back to the truck by torchlight at the end of our tethers, but the Sorcerer didn't disappoint.

Truck stuck in creek NG
Mark Garthwaite walks in to
The Sorcerer NG
Neil after The Sorceror NG

MAJO
A BIGG

'It was clear from the start that the cauldron of wildly overhanging limestone below us had the potential to blow all previously explored DWS venues clean out of the water.'

RCA

ER SPLASH

Klem Loskott TE
Neil eating cake MR
Grant Farquhar psyched TE
Café scene NG
Tim doing the jump TE
Majorcan pipe player NG
Neil off Ejector Seat, F7c MR

COVA DEL DIABLO (Neil)

We just couldn't believe our eyes when the pictures of the mystery Majorcan crag came through on email. Having tracked out most of the suitable venues at home for deep water soloing, we knew it was time to start looking further afield.

And here it was, handed to us on a plate by local climber, Miguel Riera. The covering message read simply 'No one here is interested, but I think this is suitable for you Brits?' Within weeks we were running along the cliff top in anticipation of that first gaze over the edge.

Few other crags have taken our breath away like Cova del Diablo. It was clear from the start that the cauldron of wildly overhanging limestone below us had the potential to blow all previously explored DWS venues clean out of the water. The mood changed as we pondered the significance of our discovery and the initial rush of activity was followed by a notable period of procrastination. It felt as if everything we'd done so far had been in preparation for this. If Mike Robertson hadn't been the first to scramble over the edge then I swear we'd all have remained glued to the spot in awe. But Mikey's spontaneity started a stream of new routing activity that surpassed our wildest expectations. From giant jug-fest roofs to leaning pockety walls, Diablo produced replicas of some of the finest sport climbs we'd ever done; but with the added dimension of pushing onsight into new territory with just the Mediterranean Sea for back-up. We'd hate to say that our climbing travelogue ended here, but we haven't managed to find a better crag since. So there's a challenge for you!

Fiest Queen, E5/F6b+, Lighthouse crag
Mike Robertson, 1st ascent NG

Never one to let shallow water stop play, Mike Robertson set off up the 60 ft high, leaning brown prow below the lighthouse, and everyone looked away. Mike, who was crazily psyched but without fitness after an injury lay-off, reckoned that he could clear the wave-cut platform below the route if he jumped back far enough. A slip however would be another matter. He finished the job and extolled the virtues of Fiest Queen so vigorously that we felt obliged to follow suit.

Gav Symonds on Lobster, F7a and Neil attempting 1st asc of Ejector Seat, F7c at Cova Diablo NG

'It felt as if everything we'd done so far had been in preparation for this.'

AFROMAN

Martin Atkinson on
Afroman, F7b+ NG
Martin Atkinson on
Afroman, F7b+ TE

Afroman F7b+, Cova del Diablo
Tim, 1st ascent

'Hey Tim, we could go out there!' Klem Loskot set off across the roof of the cave before taking a 30 ft plunge into the jaws of the ravenous Mediterranean. My turn. 'Go left Tim, go left! There are some pockets', Klem roared from the water. Knowing that he'd climbed French 9a, I didn't fancy my chances much but ventured out across the roof. 'Left Tim, go left', he boomed again. I couldn't believe it, the holds were just right, so beautifully positioned. What a wicked line. Go on mate, keep it together - I spurred myself on, drowned out only by the shouts of encouragement. I arrived at the finishing ledge just below the top, ditched my chalk bag and leapt into the Blue to celebrate one of the best routes ever.

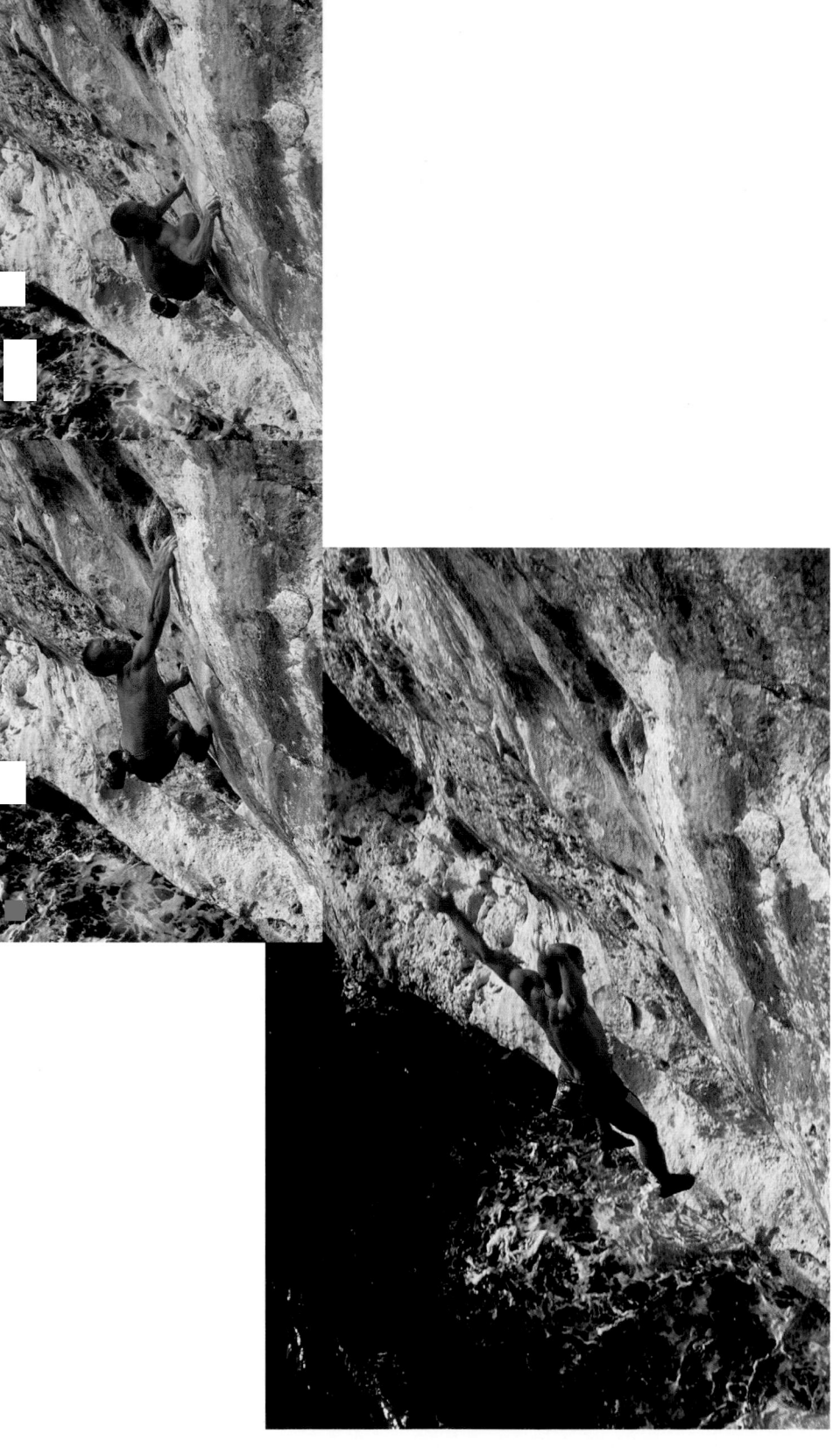

EJECTO

'It feels like going on stage, but with the world's most supportive audience behind me.'

Ejector Seat F7c, Cova del Diablo
Neil, 1st ascent MR

The timing couldn't have been better. Here I am in Majorca running desperately for the toilet when I've just found the best DWS project of my life and I'm due to fly home tomorrow. Out of options, I check into a hotel and take a valium pill. After twelve hours of sleep I return, dazed and confused, to rejoin the carnival on the cliff top. Everyone knew what I had come for. As I abseil in, it feels like going on stage, but with the world's most supportive audience behind me. I dither on the easy sea level traverse and wonder how I'm ever going to summon the firepower to dispatch the bulging orange wall above me. A brief moment of composure and then I swing up onto the line of chalked pockets. At forty feet, I can feel the eyes on my back willing me on as I reach the high point of all previous attempts - a full-arm-span dyno to gain the crucial exit holds. It's hard enough to let go mentally in these situations, let alone physically and my urge to keep things under control on previous tries had caused me to stop just short of the target. I take a sight reading, then look away, recoil and explode. But this time the friction bites into my hand and I realise that I'm still hanging there. I grip on five times harder than I need to for the final moves just to make sure I don't pour all my hard work back into the sea. Emerging from the shadows, I squint to see twenty smiling faces greeting me as I pull over top.

R SEAT

Klem Loskott latches the dyno on 1st asc of Loskott & Two Smoking Barrels, F8a+ TE

'From giant jug-fest roofs to leaning pockety walls, Diablo produced replicas of some of the finest sport climbs we'd ever done.'

LOSKOTT & TWO
SMOKING BARRELS

Jump from top of Fiest Queen, 60ft
Tim NG

The cheeky, boyish grin that so often characterised Mike Robertson's face had transformed into a somber and intense expression. Déjà vu, or what? The last time this happened he pioneered the jump from the top of Lulworth Cove in Dorset: 80 feet into only 4 metres of water. I'd followed him in, and as we walked back to the car, water ran uncontrollably down my shorts from the enema that I'd suffered. So this time I was slightly concerned. 'Right, err, OK here goes..!' The run up was perfect, and with no time to think I ejected into space. God it was high, don't look down, down, look down... SMACK. Neil followed. We all surfaced with jubilant but quizzical smiles, nurturing the parts that hurt the most.

MONG
ENDLE

'We would be in for more than you find on the average trip to Stanage.'

SS HORIZON

Horsemen NG
Team in tent NG
Fleece party NG
Horse carcass NG
Ger shelter MR
Girl portrait NG

RAIDERS OF THE LOST GRIT (Neil)

A third hand rumour from Johnny Dawes that there was gritstone in Mongolia was hardly a stable basis upon which to plan an expedition,

but with home grit being out of bounds due to foot and mouth disease it seemed like an idea worth pursuing. The Lonely Planet guide promised temperatures ranging from –45 to +45. This, combined with tales of bubonic plague and perilous mudslide roads terrorised by drunk drivers, made us realise that we would be in for more than you find on the average trip to Stanage. But we joined forces with Grant Farquhar, Seb Grieve and Mike Robertson and booked our flights to Ulan Baatar.

'Swarming mosquitos that can kill cattle and an exclusive diet of mutton and horse milk.'

Chess with Gal the Master NG
Seb Grieve and graffiti MR
Mike Robertson in the truck MR
Team with the truck MR
Grant Farquhar makes a friend MR

'A blond curly-haired guy in a Hawaiian shirt and bright yellow trousers would stand out a mile. And that was the problem.'

WAITING FOR GODOT (Neil)

It had all felt a bit too good to be true, but then the alcohol must have been stifling the warning bells.

Here we are in the early hours in a seedy back street bar in Ulan Baatar with a bunch of local wise guys who'd intercepted us as we staggered out of a night club. We should have sensed something was amiss when they wouldn't let us pay for the taxi or the first two rounds of drinks. But I came to my senses at about 5am and started gesturing to Tim and Grant that maybe we should settle our debts and split. I felt uneasy as I got to my feet and the taller guy with the leather jacket glared at me and waved me back into my seat emphatically. I smiled awkwardly and offered a round of drinks to excuse my departure but it only seemed to provoke him further. Grant and Tim were well away, absorbed in some debate and I was concerned that they'd failed to notice the rising air of hostility. Do I drag them out or leave them to it? Damn it, they're big boys - I'm going to my bed. The tall guy acknowledged my departure with a stony glare.

UB was frighteningly desolate as I tried to make sense of things from the back of the taxi. Surely it was fine and the vodka was tampering with my judgment? I crept into our apartment and drifted off to sleep.

I awoke the next morning to the sounds of Mike and Seb frantically shipping bags out of the room. Their excitement for our departure was infectious and I snapped out of my hangover and staggered to assist them. It wasn't until Seb pointed out that, predictably, we were two members of our team short that the penny dropped. Where the hell were they? Mike and Seb's immediate reaction was to be annoyed: with Gal our guide waiting in the truck, it was out of line that they were still missing in action. Mine on the other hand was much more of concern, and I explained how I'd come to be separated from Tim and Grant. 'They'll be fine. They've probably gone back to some westy's house to drink more vodka, or to a café to sober up', said Mike. 'It's a bit out of order, though'.

We made our way to the café next door for some stewed coffee and a stale bun and then sat on the dusty kerb in thick heat watching the chaos of UB in full flight. My head was pounding and Gal was looking slightly bemused. An hour passed. We apologised for the delay but were struggling to come up with an explanation. They knew how keen we all were for an early start on the first day of our journey; but it had reached 11am and still no sign. Just as we were really starting to lose our rags, Grant appeared looking hot and dishevelled. There had, of course, been a scene and he had, of course, lost Tim; but when the rest of the story unfolded we couldn't believe our ears. They had demanded a ridiculous figure for the bar bill and the tall guy had produced a knife when Tim and Grant could only rustle together fifty dollars between them. So they were bundled into a car and escorted to a cashpoint. In the back of the car, Tim and Grant had hatched a plan to dive out as it stopped at some lights, but it had gone horribly wrong and Tim was grabbed and pulled back in. Grant had watched helplessly as the car sped off knowing that Tim didn't have a cash card. We were all silent.

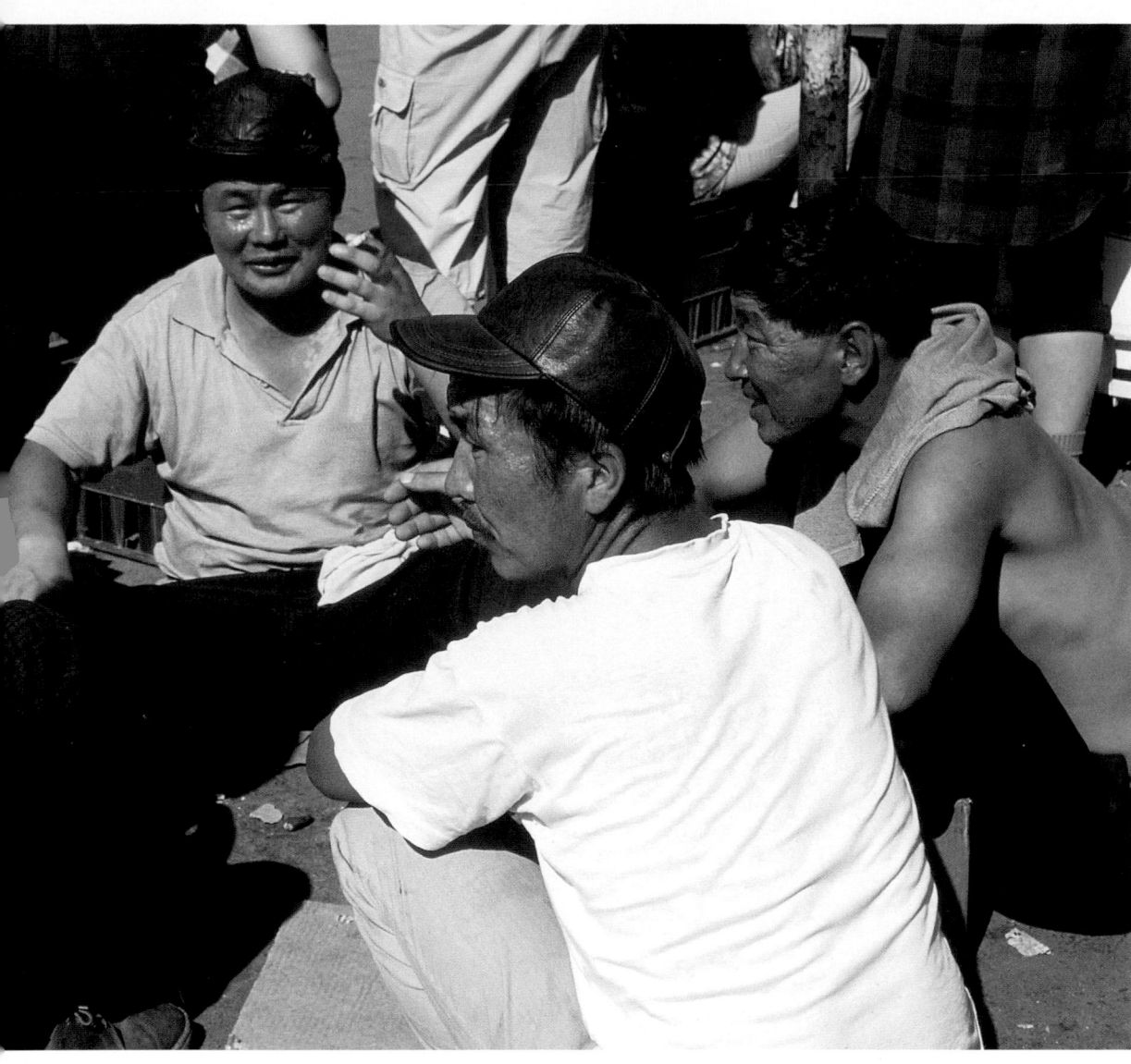

Ulan Baatar street scene NG
Mongolian police car MR

'Let's give him an hour and then ask Gal to call the police.' An hour passed. We were pretty embarrassed about our performance, but Tim's safety had to take place over our pride, so we bit the bullet and told our host what was happening. Gal was straight on the phone to the police who told him not to waste their time. Next were the taxi companies: a blond curly-haired guy in a Hawaiian shirt and bright yellow trousers would stand out a mile. And that was the problem: he had gone out last night looking like a walking target. Oh, the powers of hindsight. Next, on a more serious note, were the two city hospitals, but again, no joy. The people in the hotel reception were starting to look concerned now too, and I was trying to put the image of my friend bleeding to death in an alleyway out of my head. For the next hour there was a lot of pacing around and heated debate interspersed by periods of poignant silence. As the clock ticked we all felt that the result we were longing for was slipping away, but no one wanted to admit it. It wasn't until Seb had the courage to say what we'd all been thinking that it really hit home. Between the lot of us, we couldn't come up with a single plausible scenario that could bring Tim back to us in one piece. We had extended and extended the realistic time deadline to the point where we'd all completely lost hope. It was 1 o'clock in the afternoon. I held back the tears as I shuddered to think how we would tell his parents.

I hate myself for not dragging them out of there. I hate myself for going out on frivolous drinking nights. My whole body is trying to vomit out the impending truth. I've lost friends and family before, but not Tim. This just wasn't the right outcome for him. How can you just snuff out so much energy? The images of Tim lying there, twitching in a pool of blood were getting stronger and flashing faster in front of my eyes to the point where I was about to keel over with nausea. And just as they seemed to reach a crescendo, a taxi pulled up right in front of us outside the hotel. And there he was, like an apparition. Tim floated outwards in a slow motion haze like the last survivor in a spaghetti western shoot out; trousers torn to shreds, shirt missing, soaked in sweat and wild eyes on fire. Not one of us thought for a second to be angry or ask how or why. All we cared about was that we had our friend back. But as for what happened out there between his separation from Grant and his safe arrival at the hotel – some stories are best left untold.

'They had demanded a ridiculous figure for the bar bill and the tall guy had produced a knife when Tim and Grant could only rustle together fifty dollars between them.'

'The next day we set to work feasting on every perfect crack, dihedral and slab that came to hand.'

ENDLESS HORIZON (Neil)

We finally made it out of the city in our rickety camper van but still weren't quite sure where we were going.

Dawes had said that the gritstone could be found after a day's travel from the city, but he didn't know in which direction or by what mode of transport! So we spun the dice and after exactly a day's drive eastwards we stumbled across an area called Ghorki National Park which revealed a maze of perfectly formed rough brown domes and boulders as far as the eye could see, which on closer inspection, were clearly all made of granite. We pitched camp and were greeted almost immediately by some nomadic tribesmen who insisted on allowing us to use their horses to go new route hunting. I cantered off sideways and then immediately ground to a halt. After an hour's war of attrition and being systematically pummelled by a wooden saddle, I had inspected less than two crags and was now barely capable of standing, let alone climbing.

The next day we set to work feasting on every perfect crack, dihedral and slab that came to hand, but it was always in the back of our minds that it wasn't what we'd come to do. It took a day of debate and all our will power to tear ourselves away and hit the road, but our search for the elusive grit had to continue.

Tim teaching slacklining MR
Neil on Richard Ger, E3 5b, Ghorki Park MR
Neil on horse MR
Sapphire Crag NG

**Sapphire Crack
E5 6b, Ghorki Park,**
Neil, 1st ascent MR

I simply had to name a route after the extraordinary Sapphire Nightclub that we found in Ulan Baatar. On arrival you're shown to a table on the side of the dance floor and then invited by a compére to dance to a medley of thrash metal, 80s pop, Euro techno and traditional Mongolian music. This is interspersed with 'cool-off' periods where you are ushered back to your seats to watch entertainments which range from fire breathing to strip shows. The route features a delicious crack that eats both wires and fingers and is peppered with crazy conglomerate footholds, but it's still tedious in comparison to its namesake!

SAPPHIRE CRACK

'A delicious crack that eats both wires and fingers.'

Thunderdome and tents NG

Westworld, E6 6b, Tsetserleg,
Tim, 1st ascent MR

After days of driving around without seeing a single crag, we dived out of the truck and teemed around the mass of rocks before us. There were new lines all over the place, but on the skyline an overhanging prow caught my eye. The anticipation was killing me as I ran up the hill. What would it be like? Would there be any holds? A closer look showed that it connected. I was so psyched. Like a mini Meshuga but slightly easier and with gear. Two hand placed pegs later and I was tying in ready to do the deed, all until Seb suggested I yanked on them with a rope to test them from the ground. I went flat on my back as they both popped out. I don't fancy a Mongolian hospital. Hmmm, anyone got a hammer? The ascent was made, closely followed by team repeats, including an edge-of-the-seat performance from Mike Robertson.

WESTWORLD

Tim on Yak NG
Fish-gutting masterclass! MR
Seb shaving NG
Thunderdome and clouds NG

'There were new lines all over
the place, but on the skyline an
overhanging prow caught my eye.'

**Genghis Power,
V9, Tetseleg,**
Neil, 1st ascent   MR

We'd been away from
civilisation for too long and I
was starting to question my
sanity after spending a whole
day sitting in the dirt trying to
climb a ten foot high boulder in
the middle of Outer Mongolia.
Not being much of a boulderer,
this is probably one of the
hardest problems I've ever done
and I felt a strange sense of
loss as we drove away, knowing
that I'd never see it again.

POWER

'I was starting to question my sanity after spending a whole day sitting in the dirt.'

Neil on Dose of the Runnels,
E2 5b, 1st asc, Ghorki Park MR
Neil on horse MR

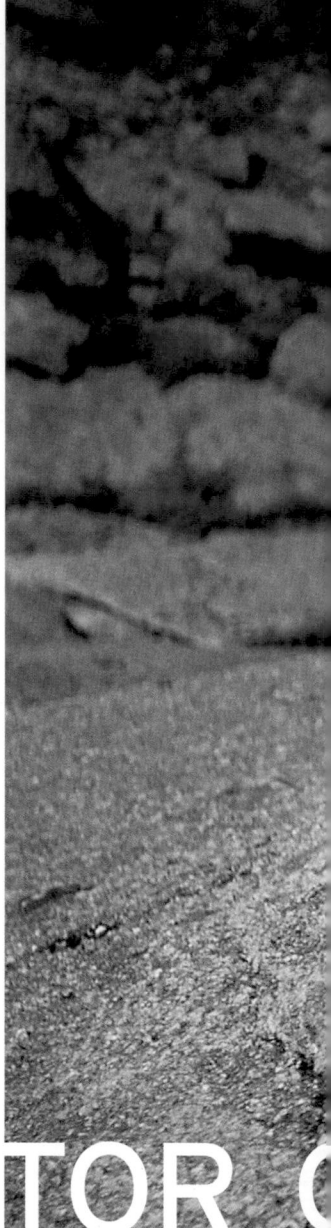

Motor Goat,
E4 5c, Ghorki Park
Tim, 1st ascent MR

This two pitch gem climbs the largest golden granite dome that we found in Gorki Park. Seb and I maintained our Mongolian onsight, ground up theme to tackle the main line of weakness on the front face. Sitting in our ancient Russian truck on the way back, we were thinking about a name for our new route and discussing the day's antics. Then, as if by magic, a motorbike started overtaking us co-piloted by a live goat! Mongolia really is a strange place.

MOTOR G

Dreaming of
Dinosaurs, E5 5c,
Ghorki Park
Tim, 1st ascent MR

As our truck dropped into the next valley, we scanned the horizon and couldn't believe our eyes. Life sized replica dinosaurs were scattered across the moraine in front of us in all directions! It just didn't make sense, this had to be one of the least popular tourist destinations in the world and yet someone had set up a dinosaur park! That night I had a dream of being chased by a 50 ft dinosaur and the next morning, as I set out on the first ascent of this poorly protected slab route, it all came back to me, 50 ft above my last piece of protection!

AT

Tents and team MR

'It took a day of debate and all our will power to tear ourselves away and hit the road, but our search for the elusive grit had to continue.'

Ulan Battered, E5 6b, Ghorki Park
Neil, 1st ascent MR

I was almost becoming complacent as I scoured the contours of yet another perfect granite wall, knowing that it would soon reveal another project to get stuck into. And then as I saw it. Why did it have to be me who found this one? Above me loomed an overhanging barrel, spliced by the meanest looking off-width crack I'd seen outside Yosemite. You know when you discover something like this that it's your duty to climb it, but you secretly wish that your friend had seen it first. 'If you're not up for it, I am!' exclaimed Tim, which only made things worse! Ulan Battered spat me out unceremoniously on at least four occasions, before I collapsed eventually on its summit. Tim's second ascent came after a similarly brutal battle.

ULAN BATTE

'Our game of pretending the gritstone would appear over the next horizon was starting to wear thin.'

We journeyed west for a week scouring endless barren plains for any signs of rock. But all that appeared were a few ancient temples and a monument to Genghis Khan. We watched the horsemen at work with their herds and ate with a family in a traditional Ger shelter, a decision which our stomachs paid for dearly over the next two days. We were taught to catch fish by elderly tribesmen as we camped by a lake in grizzly conditions that resembled Scotland. But not a sign of our beloved grit.

By the time we reached the final leg of our journey back to the capital, our game of pretending the gritstone would appear over the next horizon was starting to wear thin. A sense of anticlimax prevailed during our farewell meal at Gal's apartment, and our host sensed our disappointment in spite of the language barrier. Just as we were polishing off the last of the vodka, Gal disappeared and returned with a small geology collection that he had compiled during his travels throughout his homeland. And there it was: a rough, brown and perfectly formed specimen that could have been picked up in the Peak District. And needless to say, he couldn't remember where he found it. In this age where technology brings us so much understanding, it's nice to know that there are some secrets out there still to be unearthed.

Truck on the
endless dirt road NG
Lizard and Rocks MR

CANADA

'Where there's no blood, there's no feeling. I pitied him as the hot aches kicked in.'

Neil on Montmerancy Falls IP
Ice curtain IP
Quebec streets NG
Tim, Garth and Sandie Ogilvie
on the ferry NG

EEZE DRIED
AST

'Leashless and free, we became consumed by the reasons
we love climbing so much.'

Hot tub IP
Sandy Ogilvie and burger NG
Neil ice bouldering IP
Mark Garthwaite at airport NG
Quebec streets NG

**Mr Hyde, M7+,
Pont Rouge**
Neil IP

From rock to ice, then back
to rock again. Except at Pont
Rouge, there's nowhere to hide
- the fragile hanging daggers
actually feel more secure than
the rock to which they are
somehow bonded. Each ledge
creaks unnervingly under the
strain of my picks and I'm loath
to have a bucket of rubble
dumped in my face. Worse
is the thought of testing the
bolts - only a few days ago, one
pulled out on a local climber,
still attached to a TV set-sized
block of shale!

MR HYDE

'Each ledge creaks unnervingly under the
strain of my picks and I'm loath to have a
bucket of rubble dumped in my face.'

LA POMME D'OR (Tim)

Saturday night and Quebec
city was in full carnival mode after the
final of the Ice World Cup. 'You know
there'll be no pity from me if you two
go clubbing tonight - we're leaving first
thing for Pomme D'Or, regardless of
your sorry states!'

Garth made himself clear that we had a
schedule to maintain.

At 6am on Sunday morning, light poured into the
narrow corridor as I opened the exit door to the
club. Neil and I stood there in total disbelief after
the best night in a long while. With a foot of fresh
powder covering the streets, the taxi driver treated
us to a Colin McCrae-style rally drive home, which
was as memorable as the night itself. Garth took
great pleasure in bundling us sleepless into the truck
outside the youth hostel, and we set off north,
up the coast.

The next morning we staggered out of our hostel at
5am. It was still dark and the temperature was -30
C. I watched as Garth, Neil, Sandy and Ian squeezed
on board our new mode of transport – the sledge.
They were packed in like a lavish harvest of Santa's
presents, wearing every item of clothing they
possessed and huddled in their sleeping bags as
they braced with trepidation for the ride. I jumped
on the back of the skidoo behind the driver, and
we set off. We had 35km to go. The driver's fingers
clutched tightly onto the metal accelerator lever as
we absconded into the darkness on our quest for the
'Golden Apple'.

Half an hour later we stopped, and the driver
dismounted the skidoo and started hopping around
shaking his frozen hands. Where there's no blood,
there's no feeling. I pitied him as a pained expression
came over his face. The familiar signs of the hot
aches kicked in as the blood started pulsing into his
constricted capillaries, bursting them open and back
to life. Neil appeared to be frozen solid in his sleeping
bag. The stars retreated from the illuminated sky and
the 1000 ft frozen monolith came into view.
It looked amazing.

Sandy de-icing NG
No room for us NG
Neil sleeping IP
Team and skidoo NG
Crossing the frozen lake NG
Tim belaying Garth on
Pomme D'Or, WI 6, pitch 4 IP

LA POMME

Garth on Pomme D'Or WI 6, pitch 4 IP
Tim on Pomme D'Or, pitch 5 IP
Tim on Pomme D'Or, pitch 5 IP

'It was heaven - even the sun sparkled intermittently on the glowing flutings.'

Testing our primitive grasp of French, we had arranged a pick-up 10 hours later, and there was only one thing between us and the start of the route - the lake! The driver gestured that we walk straight across, but the peculiar cracks and bubble formations in the ice inspired little confidence. We soon arrived at the base and were unable to put our crampons on fast enough. After a few grade 3 and 4 pitches we began our assault of the main 200 metres of vertical golden ice which give the route its name. It was heaven - even the sun sparkled intermittently on the glowing flutings. Our only concern was that the crux pillar had become completely detached at its base. It looked extremely fragile and there was no way I would be able to place screws for at least the first forty feet. After a few deep breaths, I set out moving as lightly as possible over thin chandeliers with a thousand feet of space below. But I was soon winding in the screws for the belay below the final headwall. Garth led through and it was vertical nearly all the way. Leashless and free, we became consumed by the reasons we love climbing so much, and in the haze of the failing light, we flopped over the top.

Revenge was sweet on the descent as Neil and I heard the echo of Garth's shouts up behind us as he abseiled into the darkness to find his ropes entwined in a plethora of icy bushes. We chuckled as we ran ahead in search of the best position on the homebound chariot, still electrified from the day's experience. Later that night, the owner of the hostel treated us to the most bountiful meal we had encountered since our arrival in Quebec. Or maybe we were still salivating after sampling the tastier fruits of La Pomme D'or.

D'OR

Montmerancy Falls, WI 3, Quebec
Neil IP

Few ice climbs come with the novelty value of Montmerancy Falls. For a start, they are a short bus ride from the city centre of Quebec, which makes them the perfect hangover cure after a night on the town. Secondly, they can be climbed at any time of day or night owing to the spectacular floodlights that illuminate them after dusk. And finally they can be climbed at whatever grade you want, depending on which line you take. But however or whenever you climb them, the deafening thunder of the falls will remain in your ears and the spray will keep stinging your eyes long after the ascent is complete.

'The deafening thunder of the falls will remain in your ears.'

MONTMERANCY FALLS

'Life's too short for
redpointing.'

CUBA
VIVA LA
REVOLUCI

VIVA LA REVOLUCI

PARTICULAR
PM·01189
CUBA

ON

Rum glasses MR
Girl in Havana MR
Old lady and cigar MR
Team with Mrs Miggins NG
Car fender NG
Pierced Westy MR
Palm tree and beach MR
Farmer in field MR

Seb Grieve, taxi and cigar NG
Team on beach NG
Old men and car NG
Charlie Woodburn top roping a
new line on Cuba Libra crag NG
Anna Griessing bouldering
near Vinales MR

'I reeled out a load of rope and held my breath...'

¡VIVA LA REVOLUCION VICTORIOSA EN EL NUEVO MILENIO!

Viva La Revolucion NG
Charlie Woodburn on
Mr Nice, F7c, 1st asc MR
Mike walks in to the crag NG
Wasp nest NG
Mike Roberston ground-up
equipping the Wasp Factory,
F7b, Vinales SG

MR NICE

'Within arm's reach of Mike, every spare inch of rock was encrusted with evil hanging nests.'

THE WASP FACTORY (Neil)

'Seriously now, how much do you want this one, Neil?' said Mike Roberston.
'Err, quite a lot, I think mate.'
'Right, well we're going to have to go for it then, aren't we?'
'Are you sure you're alright to - '

Before I could dissuade him, Mike was off. A huge wave of limestone reared over our heads at a continuous angle of 45 degrees, its underside riddled with tufas and stalactites. Our target was to bolt our way up to the giant dangling phallus at 60 feet and from there onwards to the top. Bolting on abseil simply isn't an option in Cuba - not even Indiana Jones would make it through the poison ivy infested jungle that surrounds every worthwhile piece of rock. So with our cordless Hilti connected to a zip line, and full aiding apparel, Mikey set to it. At this stage it was much easier to ignore the fact that the limestone to the right of our line was that nice familiar orangey grey colour and the limestone to its left was a rather alien looking browny black. The reason for this was because our chosen line deliminated the boundary of the world's largest wasp nest! Within arm's reach of Mike, every spare inch of rock was encrusted with evil hanging nests, some of them abandoned, but most of them alive and swarming. Mikey freed a move or two, placed a rattly wire in a pocket and then threw a sling round a tufa pipe. 'OK - take me there and send her up.' We'd tested the drill for volume and resonance at ground level and we hadn't disturbed the wasps, but Mikey was closer now. 'Get ready to lower', he muttered. Deep breath, and the first anchor went in.

I noticed that the higher he proceeded from here, the closer our route was getting to the black line. At 50 feet they started circling him. Mike placed a sky hook in a tiny pocket and surveyed the scene.
'I need to drill about 4 inches from a nest
- it's not going to happen.'
'OK, sack it, it's not worth it. I'll lower you.'
'Hang on wait... maybe.'
'Don't risk it mate.'
'Sod it, let's have a go - if they attack, I'll pop the hook. Give me loads of slack!'

I reeled out a load of rope and held my breath as I heard the noise of the drill; but within seconds Mike let out a cry and came hurtling downwards, drill still in hand. I caught him after about 30 feet but immediately continued lowering him, at a pace not much less than the fall itself. A small black cloud descended after him but then seemed to dissipate. We sprinted back from the crag, ropes, clutter and all, until we realised that we were no longer being chased. Mike's eyelid had completely closed after a target hit so I set to sucking the sting out before it got any worse. 'All yours, Neil. Over to you!'

That night, I gathered together every piece of protective clothing we owned from the team and I returned the next day to sweat it out in the full sun to finish the bolting. Two days later the clothing was removed long enough for a successful free ascent of 'The Colony' 8a+ to be made. Anyone who's dabbled with redpoint style sport climbing knows how important it is to be focused on the moves. The slightest disturbance and all sorts of things can happen.

Neil sucks wasp sting from
Mike Robertson's eye! MR
The Exterminator Suit! MR
Neil jummaring up to equip
The Colony MR

'The slightest
disturbance and all sorts
of things can happen.'

COLONY

The Colony 8a+, Vinales
Neil, 1st ascent MR

The wall reared over even more steeply above the huge stalactite where we had finished the Wasp Factory and the obvious challenge still remained: to free climb the entire wave from bottom to top. I returned to bolt and practise the extension, which revealed a vicious boulder problem crux. It was all I could do to hang the holds on first acquaintance but the usual redpointing persistence paid dividends. Whilst all this was going on, Tim and I were having salsa dancing lessons in the evenings with our pal Abel from the village, who could move like greased lightning. But this was one sequence we were destined never to get wired.

'I wanted to be part of the
team again, not locked away
by my project, ostracised
from their antics.'

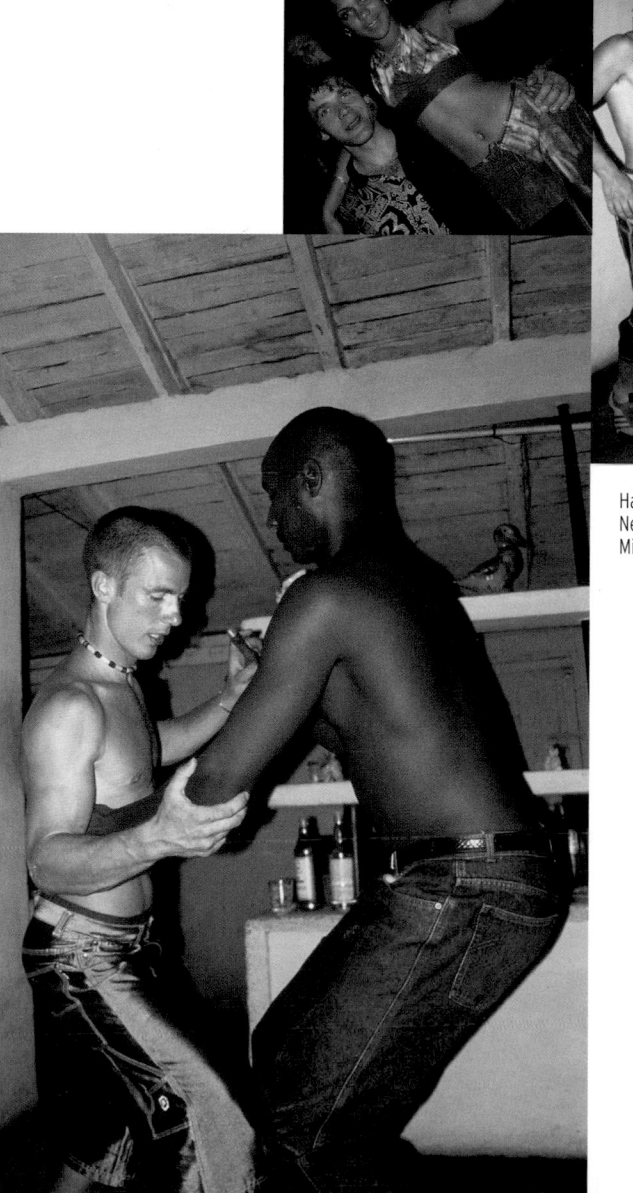

Havana street scene MR
Neil learning to Salsa TE
Mike Robertson hones his skills NG

Have a Cigar, 8a
Neil, 1st free ascent MR

Full credit to visiting American
pioneer Craig Leuben for equipping
and climbing out from the depths
of this gloomy cave along a
remarkable downward pointing
'bat's wing' shaped fin of rock.
Less style points to him for using
a ladder to miss out the first hard
section! Some extra bolts were
placed and the whole thing went
free courtesy of some acrobatics.
A climb that defies logic in the
sense that it seems to lose more
height than it gains.

THE ONE INCH PUNCH, F8b (Tim)

I'd always said that life was too short for redpointing. And there I was in Cuba having spent the entire trip trying to climb the same piece of rock while the rest of the team were on tour.

I had bolted a 30m pitch up an incredible wave of tufa-covered limestone and I had fallen off the same move only a few feet from the lower-off sixteen times now. I felt dazed, confused and totally battered. I had even stayed in while the others partied the last three nights away with our local friends in Vinales. This alone took more strength than you might believe. Tomorrow we were leaving, and tonight I had to go out. I wanted to be part of the team again, not locked away by my project, and ostracised from their antics. I needed a release.

3am the next morning: 'Tim, get off the roof! It'll collapse', Neil ushered me down from my rickety perch on top of the bar where we'd been drinking all night. The 'Cuba Libras' were giving me more

'Dehydration had got the better of me and I felt really light!'

THE ONI

Abel - Salsa Doctor TE
Coconut tree NG
Team by taxi NG
Tim, The One Inch Punch, F8b,
Vinales, 1st asc MR

NCH PUNCH

than the desired effect as Seb picked me up off the floor and helped me home. The next morning I was dehydrated, my head was cloudy but my mind at last was set at ease from redpoint torture. There was no way it could happen now. But I still had to retrieve the quickdraws and Mike was also keen to get pictures as a momento of our efforts, so we headed off towards the crag.

As Mikey jummared into position, I warmed up on Neil's route, the 'Wasp Factory', and tried a few moves on the extension, 'the Colony', just to get myself going a bit. I looked up at my project one last time. I had to get to the top of it to get the draws, so I might as well have one last go. I had nothing to

lose and I was too hung-over to contemplate being nervous. I tied into the 8mm rope I'd been using to reduce drag and set off. Dehydration had got the better of me and I felt really light! I didn't have to think as it was all programmed into the system. A few moves from the crux, I was aware of Mikey right next to me snapping away and luring me onwards with his soft tones: 'Go on Tim, go on mate.' The move that had been stopping me involved a rapid-fire snatch for a close range pocket, requiring the speed and accuracy of a Bruce Lee martial arts manoeuvre. I set up and released. Two fingers hit the hole like John Redhead could have only dreamed of. You beauty! I clipped the lower off and the 'One Inch Punch' was reincarnated in the last hour.

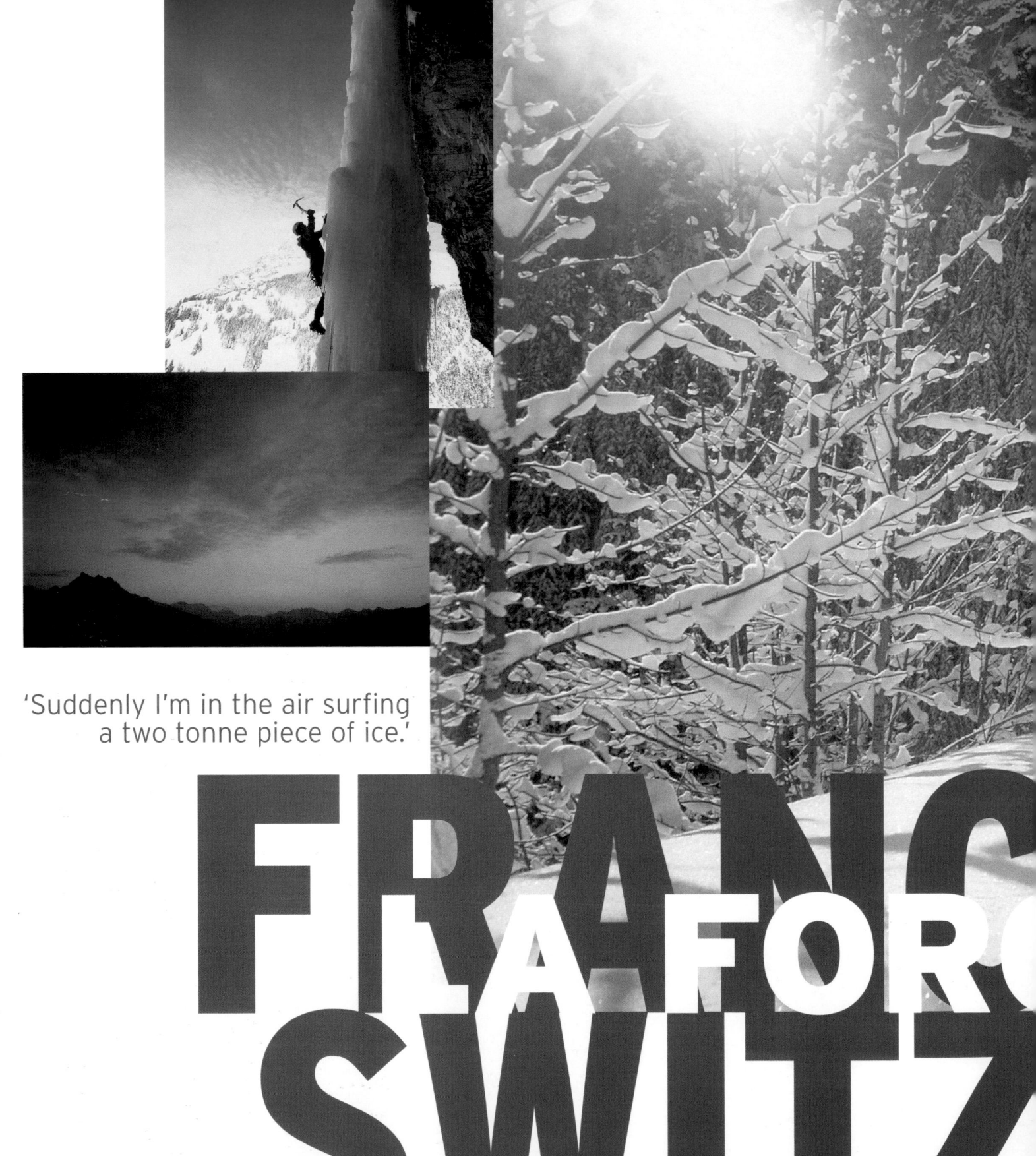

'Suddenly I'm in the air surfing
a two tonne piece of ice.'

FRANC
LA FOR
SWITZ

Neil on Reise Integral,
WI 6, Kandersteg IP
Mountain sunset NG
Neil skiing skiing up to
Oeschinenwald, Kandersteg NG
Rooftop icicles NG

E TRANQUIL
ERLAND

'Water ice grades (prefixed WI) go from 1 to 6 according to the gradient of the climb, with 1 being an easy-angled slab and 6 being continuously vertical.

Ice rarely gets steeper than vertical and hence grade 7 applies to thin, fragile features which are prone to collapse.' (Guidebook quote)

Ten feet above a rotten old peg, crampon points balancing on rock, I breathe in and gently tap the icicle. It flexes and makes a dull booming sound. Don't hit it, don't hit it. Hook my right pick in a tiny air pocket. Still there. Left axe just above - OK this is it now - transfer. Be as light as possible. Right mono-point on a dimple and CRAACKKKK! Suddenly I'm in the air surfing a two tonne piece of ice. The rope pulls tight and flicks me in just above a ledge and the plummeting ice block splits across my thigh.

A moment to regroup and make gasping noises. At least it's only my leg that's dead - I haven't had one like this since school days. Above me, only half of the ice feature remains, its base now blunt and truncated at the fracture point. Surely the fact that my climb no longer exists counts as acceptable circumstances for quitting? 'Maybe you could dry-tool back up and join the fun a bit higher?' suggested Ian Parnell. 'You're having a laugh! Or maybe...' Yes, no, yes, no, yes, no. 'Go on then, let's have a look...'

Second time up, I'm definitely too high above that peg to miss the ledge now. The tell-tale scratch marks on the rock have run out and I'm a move short of fat Freddy. Maybe I could just stretch a little higher and get an axe – PING! one of my crampon points flies off, causing me to barn-door outwards, but my solitary pick remain seated on a verglassed edge and I'm still on. Shit, it's got to be the move then. Deep breath. A high step to a verglassed foothold and a sideways torque. Extend and it's looming in the corner of my eye. You're mine this time. The shaft of my axe reverberates, telling me all I need to know as I swing up and out.

Neil on Rise and Shine, WI 7, Kandersteg (half the route is clearly missing!) IP
Neil gearing up IP
Ian Parnell - organised alpinist! NG

'Guaranteed to make your arms pump and your heart race.'

REISE INTEGRAL

Reise Integral, WI 6,
Kandersteg, Switzerland
Neil IP

The classic ice pillar of the area is guaranteed to make
your arms pump and your heart race. Halfway up I hit
it slightly too hard and a huge block detached itself. I
braced myself for the impact, but fortunately it dropped
inwards, causing me to be drenched by a spurt of the
icy water that was running inside the tube!

'Wild, gymnastic moves using axes and crampons as replacements for hands and feet.'

PINK PANTHER

**Pink Panther, M10-,
Kandersteg, Switzerland**
Neil IP

The modern style of bolted 'dry
tooling' has opened new frontiers in
winter climbing. Rather than aiding
your way up steep, barren rock to
a suspended ice feature, you can
make wild, gymnastic moves using
axes and crampons as replacements
for hands and feet. But aesthetics
in climbing are all-important. The
true mixed lines are the ones that
use the rock as a key to access the
ice rather than an excuse for pure
technical difficulty. The ice finish on
Pink Panther is a fitting climax to the
show that goes on below.

'Stolen from under the noses of the French the day before the ski lifts opened.'

David Hesleden on pitch 2 of the first asc of Tequila Stuntman WI 6+, M6 NG
Neil on pitch 3 of the first ascent of Tequila Stuntman AP

Tequila Stuntman
WI 6, M6+, Chamonix
Tim CL

Named after a suicidal drinking game: snort a line of salt, down the tequila, then squirt the lemon in your eye! This was an absolute diamond find by the British trio - Dave Hesleden, Neil and the guru himself, Andy Parkin. Created by a diverted watercourse from an underground reservoir, this route had never previously existed and was stolen from under the noses of the French the day before the ski lifts opened at the start of the season.

TEQUILA

STUNTMAN

Escape from the Tardis! TE
Neil sets out on pitch 1 of Crack Baby,
WI 6, 340m, Kandersteg TE
Tim high on pitch 7 NG
Summit celebration! TE

CRAC

CRACK BABY (Tim)

It's essential to decide your priorities if you are to make the most of a trip away.

There were three reasons why I had come to Kandersteg: Firstly, I had heard that my friends from the Ice World Cup were going to be at the party after the ice festival and I really wanted to see them. Secondly, Lauhterbrunan, the most popular BASE jumping destination in Europe, was nearby and I had my parachute packed and ready for action. On top of that, one of the most amazing ice routes in the world, a ten pitch grade VI called Crack Baby, had come into condition, but unfortunately there was only one day left in the trip for Neil and I to attempt it. The problem was that this just happened to be the morning after the party! Neil was clearly concerned by my distractions and early that evening he came out with a right clanger: 'If you're not in your bed by midnight, I'm not doing the route with you, end of story!' I couldn't believe it. I've always used climbing to abscond from the rules and regulations of everyday life and now my climbing partner had set me a curfew. That can't be right.

That evening, I competed in the final of the competition at the festival, but it finished late at 11pm, meaning that I only had an hour to catch up with everyone afterwards. It wasn't long enough, and when I realised that Neil had arranged for Chris Cubitt to substitute me if I didn't make it back in time, I was seriously torn. As the clock struck midnight, I phoned Neil to reassure him I was on my way, but saying my farewells at a time like this took Herculean strength.

A few hours later the alarm sparked us into action and we drove off to find the cable car which we had booked for 5.30am. A narrow road up from the main valley finished at a farm by an old barn and at first we thought we'd made a mistake. The lift turned out to be antique - an oversized metal soap box with broken windows, suspended from a rusty old cable. The farmer nodded confidently, but I was amazed when it actually jolted into motion and ferried us up the mountainside through the darkness. It felt like an adventure already. Suddenly our Dr Who time machine juddered to a halt 50 metres short of the docking point. We waited for a few minutes but nothing happened, so we concluded that it had taken its final breath. Peering out of the door into the darkness, it was difficult to get a perspective of how high up we were, but it didn't look far, ten feet perhaps. 'Right then Neil, I guess we'll just have to bail out', I proposed. Neil raised his eyebrows and looked unimpressed. I jumped out and landed in a heap on the snow. It was further than I thought! Neil tentatively followed. As we set off up the hill, the white threads which outlined 1000 foot ice lines were translucent in the shadows of the giant ampitheatre above us.

As we arrived at the base, the married man Gresham proposed an armory of ice protection, fifteen screws to be exact. There was no way I was carrying that lot and like bartering for a t-shirt at a Bangkok road stall, I proposed half. We settled for ten and the next few hours blurred into a frozen haze. The last 300ft was like climbing polystyrene and our picks injected into the ice like darts into a board. Topping out, Neil was euphoric, 'Surely the best ice route we'd ever done?' He always says that. The only way I could heighten the experience would be to come back with my BASE rig and fly off the top. Now there's an idea!

'I've always used climbing to abscond from the rules and regulations of everyday life and now my climbing partner had set me a curfew.'

BABY

LA

La Dame Du Lac, WI 6, Chamonix
Tim IP

Ever since I saw the picture of Thierry Renault running it out 30 feet above his last piece of protection whilst taming the Lady of the Lake, I knew, I had to do this route. Transfixed by this image year after year, if there was one ice route in the world I wanted to do, it was definitely this one. When I heard it was in condition, I couldn't pick the phone up fast enough. 'Miles, Miles, La Dame Du Lac's in nick, let's do it, are you keen?' Miles Bright didn't need any persuasion. The next morning after an early caffeine-fuelled start, we stood at the base gazing at this incredible ice feature bounded on both sides by overhanging walls. It was so good that days later I tempted Andy Perkins and snowboarding legend Neil McNab to join me so I could return and do it again.

DAME DU LAC

'If there was one ice route in the world
I wanted to do, it was definitely this one.'

ORANGE S
THA

UNSHINE
ILAND

'It wasn't until we took a boat trip
out to explore some of the nearby islands
that the tables turned.'

'We were incredulous
that no one had yet
sampled such seemingly
obvious goods.'

ORANGE SUNSHINE (Neil)

One of our policies when it comes to climbing trips abroad is never to visit the same place twice.

But a trusted friend of ours who shares the same view has been back to Thailand three times. Although we were intrigued to find out what the fuss was all about, neither of us were in contention for any serious action when we arrived at Railay beach near Krabi. One of us (Neil) was able bodied, but his mind was recovering from a recent struggle with Equilibrium back home on the gritstone. The other, on the other hand, was chomping at the bit whilst being restrained by a shoulder injury incurred from a snowboarding collision.

Fortunately when we got there, the idea of bush-whacking through the jungle and getting savaged by mosquitos as you sweat it out on some polished sport route seemed of limited appeal. We were promptly seduced by a life of hanging out in coffee shops, slack-lining on perfect beaches, swimming in emerald clear seas, feasting on delicious seafood and then working it all off through the night at the 'full moon parties'. It wasn't until we took a boat trip out to explore some of the nearby islands that the tables turned. We had inadvertently stumbled on yet another premier deep water soloing venue and we were incredulous that no one had yet sampled such seemingly obvious goods. Each day from then on, we hired a boat and set about weaving our way up and then leaping off the multitude of limestone caves and towers that surround the bay. We'd finish up the day on a deserted sand-bar island sipping a beer as the sun dipped and set the sky on fire. At the time we thought it just couldn't get any better. But then we hadn't been to Vietnam yet!

Louise Gresham in boat
on Railay beach NG
Boatman silhouette NG
Tim onsight new routing NG

'Each day from then on, we hired a boat and set about weaving our way up and then leaping off the multitude of limestone caves and towers that surround the bay.'

Railay Bay scene NG
Woman in Bangkok NG
Tonsai jungle NG
Boatman NG
Mushroom coffee shop! NG

Spiderman, 7c+, Krabi
Neil, 1st ascent TE

One of the caves embedded within the complex coastline of Chicken Island revealed an incredible sea level traverse line, above perfect deep green water. Two hundred feet long and getting steeper and steeper all the way, but with a line of 'chicken head' jugs all the way along. I set off, yarding my way across, only to find myself in the sea after a close encounter with an angry looking poisonous spider. I took my swat rag with me the second time and settled the score and continued to finish this gem of a project. Tim made an impressive flashed second ascent and this definitely ranks as one of the top five biggest pumps I've ever had!

SPIDERMAN

'I set off, yarding my way across, only to find myself in the sea after a close encounter with an angry looking poisonous spider.'

VIETNA QU

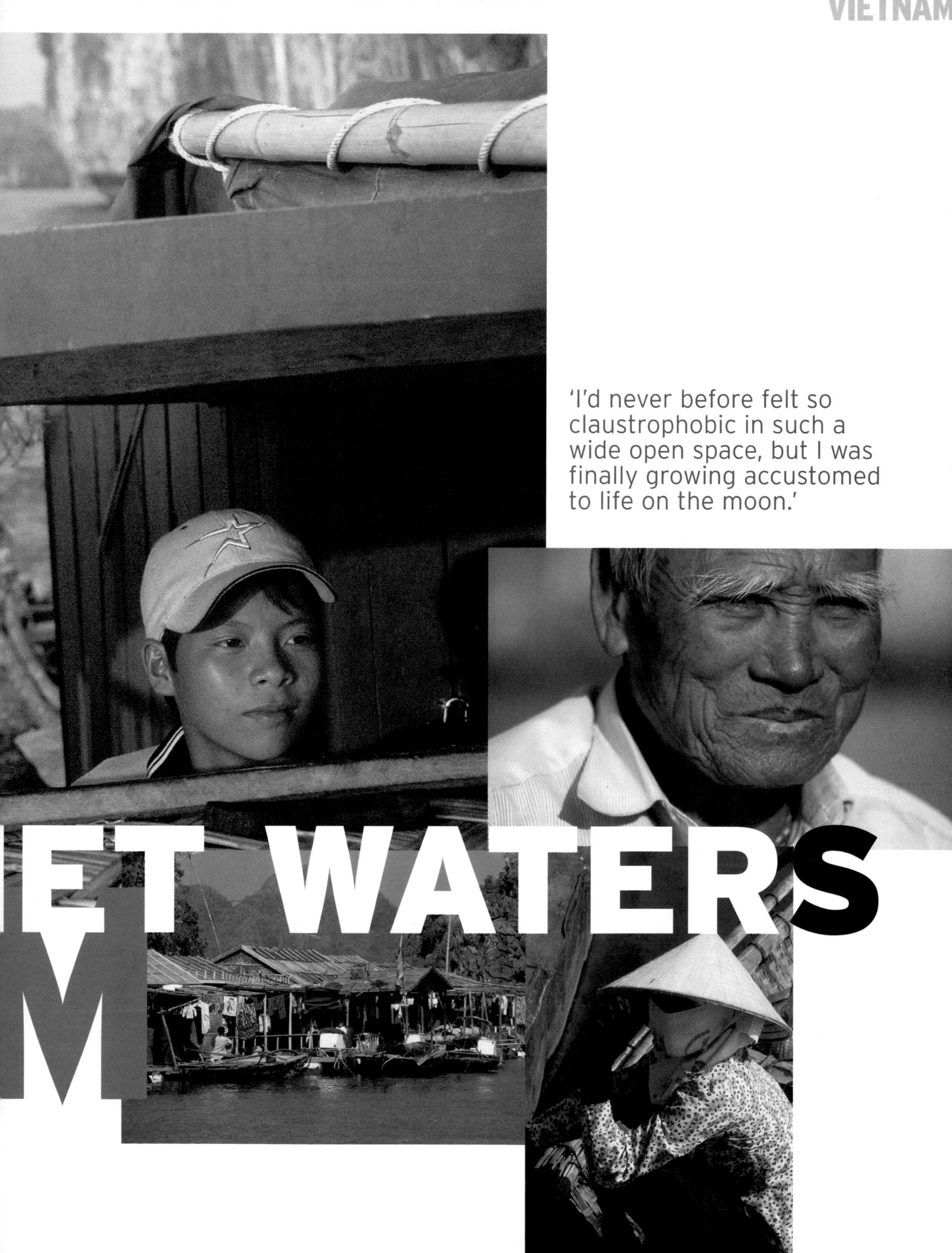

'I'd never before felt so claustrophobic in such a wide open space, but I was finally growing accustomed to life on the moon.'

ET WATERS
M

Ha Long Nights, F7a+, Ha Long Bay
Grant Farquhar, 3rd ascent NG

Grant spacewalks between stalactites on one of the most exciting deep water solos we've ever found, whilst Ting and Tang man the boat. Our inability to communicate with our friendly two-strong cabin crew proved frustrating at times. To our dismay, every evening they insisted on dragging us away from the crag well before sunset with projects still to go. Stranger still, they would cut the engine so we slowed to a crawl and then take us to some concealed cove or lagoon. We couldn't understand what was wrong with spending the night where we were, out in the open sea, and it wasn't until we opened our travel guide that it clicked. Apparently there are more active pirates in this ocean than in any other part of the world.

'They would cut the engine so we slowed to a crawl and then take us to some concealed cove or lagoon.'

Jellyfish pie TE
Tim attempting an unfinished project GF
Tim and Grant Farquhar on deck NG
Seb Grieve mends the recce boat NG

HO CHI MINH

**Ho Chi Minh, F7c+,
Halong Bay**
Neil, 1st ascent SG

After two days of falling into
the sea from the same section
of cave ceiling, Seb and I were
both relieved to have nailed our
projects. Ho Chi Minh involved
50 feet of powerful upside-down
climbing (despite gaining no more
than 20 feet in height) and a crazy
rest after the crux, hanging from
a foot jam. Seb's route 'Burgundy'
took a bouldery line just to its left
at F7b. As we sailed off we sat on
deck for a while, contemplating
the sheer bizarreness of what we
were doing and we both agreed
that we were looking forward to
seeing a little more of Vietnam.

'Relative mind is the mind that
sets itself in relation to other
things, thus limiting itself.'

Shunryu Suzuki

LION FACE

'Yesterday, we had spotted a stunning 50m high, diamond shaped, orange flowstone wall that was crying out to be made into a world class sport climb.'

NIGHTRIDER (Neil)

It was one of those moments
when I just felt completely content.
Out on the deck lying under the stars,
everything was glowing nicely after my
fifth-or-something can of beer.

During our first week on the boat, I'd never before
felt so claustrophobic in such a wide open space, but
I was finally growing accustomed to life on the moon.
Every night so far I'd been running and dancing round
the deck like a caged tiger, but tonight my sleeping
bag feels great. Oh, the joys of doing your project.

It had been the first day of the trip where we'd split
the team. Seb and I had been deep water soloing as
usual, whereas Tim and Grant had gone off on a quest
of a different nature. Although we had vowed not to
use the drill this trip, some opportunities are just too
good to pass up. Yesterday, we had spotted a stunning
50m high, diamond shaped, orange flowstone wall
that was crying out to be made into a world class
sport climb. And today Tim and Grant were putting
the bolts in. It seemed like a mammoth task in itself
just to bush-whack to the top and place the bolts;
and Seb and I had expected to return at sunset to
find them still hard at it. But instead, Grant was just
finishing off the final bolt while Tim was hopping
around, beside himself with frustration.

Seb Grieve on Lion Face,
F6c+, 1st asc NG
Neil off Rock The Cat Ba,
F7b, after 1st asc TE
Surveying the line of Nightrider
on 'Han's Island' NG

I really couldn't see the problem; OK, they hadn't had time for the free ascent today, but surely we'd simply moor up for the night somewhere nearby and return refreshed the next morning so they could finish the job?

Back to where we were - out on deck with the alcohol sending me off into a dreamy haze. Grant and Seb were already snoring. But the person to my right was still twitching with excitement at the thought of his unclimbed line.

A tap on my shoulder: 'Hey, let's have it!'
'Err, have what?' I feign ignorance, hoping to God he doesn't mean what I think he means.
'The route. Come on, for old time's sake! You know - back to the days of Central Icefall. A bit of head torch action!'
'Err – no. Go to sleep.'
'Yeah, I suppose you're right. You are past thirty now, and you're married. Best leave it, hey?'
Silence.
'I can't believe you resorted to that line, you bastard. Go on then. Let's pack the stuff.'

If nothing else, I wanted to get him off the boat because he was keeping Ting and Tang, our crew, awake. As we crept around deck gathering our kit, I felt that someone had to weigh up the situation for what it was, rather than acting purely on impulse. My main concern was that Tim was half cut, as well as the fact that we had at least a mile of rowing to do before we could even attempt this absurd prank. But then two negatives can make a positive, so I ordered Tim to row in the hope that it would sober him up...

'Yeah, I suppose you're right. You are past thirty now, and you're married. Best leave it, hey?'

Tim and Grant Farquhar are rowed in to equip Nightrider NG
Grant below Nightrider TE
Seb Grieve and Tang heckle from the deck NG

NIETZSCHE HAD IT

**Nietzsche Had It,
F7b+, Ha Long Bay**
Tim, 1st ascent NG

Halfway into our trip, an amazing arch shaped crag came into view. It seemed entirely inaccessible apart from a single hanging stalactite from which a rope had been suspended by fisherman to anchor their boats. I launched up this and then out onto a tufa pipe which breached a 45 degree leaning wall. As I battled with the steepness, willing myself onwards, two of Neitzsche's quotes seemed appropriate - 'live dangerously' and 'I will have it'. To do this, you must try harder than ever before, never give up, dig deep and hang on to the dear end. In this case I got to the top, just.

NIGHT

'I should have known better, and a sales pitch followed, in which he managed to convince me that the route was '6b+ish' and that I *had* to do it.'

DER

We steered a largely straight course to our island, and within half an hour were stumbling around in the darkness on the boulders at the base of the wall. I hit play on the stereo and Steve Lawler's beats echoed eerily as they bounced off the rock above us. A quick safety check, and before I knew it, Tim was gone up into the night. I could barely pay the rope out quickly enough and within minutes I was lowering him back down, grinning from ear to ear under his torch beam. But then just as I started to celebrate that we could go home to bed: 'Right then - your turn!'

I should have known better, and a sales pitch followed, in which he managed to convince me that the route was '6b+ish' and that I *had* to do it. I know enough about myself to realise that I am likely to be a fair way from my physical prime in the early hours of the morning when I'm drunk and I can barely see. Knowing Tim as I do, I'm aware that a completely different set of rules apply to him at times like this. But, with much trepidation, I decide to go for it anyway. I grovel and thrutch on what should be a beautifully flowing piece of climbing, and by 80 feet, I'm pumped out of my mind. Completely disorientated, I feel like I'm on a never-ending limestone treadmill, no closer to the bottom than I am to the top. Plus, in true Tim style, the bolts have been placed 'sportingly' and the route culminates in a twenty foot run-out to the belay anchor. I hear a shout from below. 'The crux is the last move - but you'll be fine!' But I'm already fifteen feet out, off line and done for. I eject backwards from my pool of light and tumble into the blackness.

We returned the next morning for a far less eventful team ascent of 'Nightrider', and I was interested, though not surprised, when it turned out to be closer to French 7b in grade. I'm sure there's a lesson to be learnt there somewhere.

Tim returning to Nightrider NG
Tim warming up on the boat NG
Tim rowes to Nightrider NG
Tim preparing kit to equip Nightrider NG
Tim on Nightrider, F7b, 1st asc NG

ICE

IWC

WORLD CUP

Neil filing IP
Quebec Tower 02 IP
Tim loving the pain,
Courchevel 00 RW
Kirov spectator TE
Kirov Crowd TE
Stephan Hussan, Pitztal 02 TE

Pitztal tower 02 TE
The first ever British ice team! 00 DP
Training with Andy Coish IP
Francois Lombard wins Pitztal 00 NG
Tim qualifies at Cortina 00 NG

'The whole notion of ice climbing
competitions seemed crazy from the start
and we soon realised that the secret is not to
take them too seriously.'

'It's not often you figure-of-4 your way across an ice roof and then hang from a heel spur to rest when you're gully bashing on Ben Nevis.'

QUEBEC

A BRAVE ATTEMPT (Neil)

Can you ever imagine how you're going to feel when you hear the four minute warning?

When the announcement was made over the intercom that it was our turn to leave the isolation area, we knew that the time had come. And our only consolation was that we were going out together. We discarded our bags and took with us only the tools and protective clothing that we needed for survival and made our way to the transit zone. We looked at each other for the final time. As the tent walls were peeled back we were hit by an icy blast and a giant white mushroom cloud reared up in front of us above the Quebec sky line.

The first World Cup series in '99 had been a comedy of errors for the 'British team'. We arrived without competition tools, only to slide ungracefully off the shafts of our Scottish style straight axes in the final of the first event in Pitztal, Austria. The second event was nearly missed when we became stranded after our keys were stolen from a nightclub in Chamonix. A white-knuckle drive across the Alps helped us make up for lost time, only to arrive in Courchevel to realise that the tower had collapsed in the night and the competition had been cancelled. There wasn't a single event that wasn't preceded by a wild party night, and we have hazy memories of French champions crawling through the snow on their hands and knees to their beds. But first place has to go to

Neil qualifies at Quebec 02 IP
Quebec Tower 02 NG
Shady spectator TE

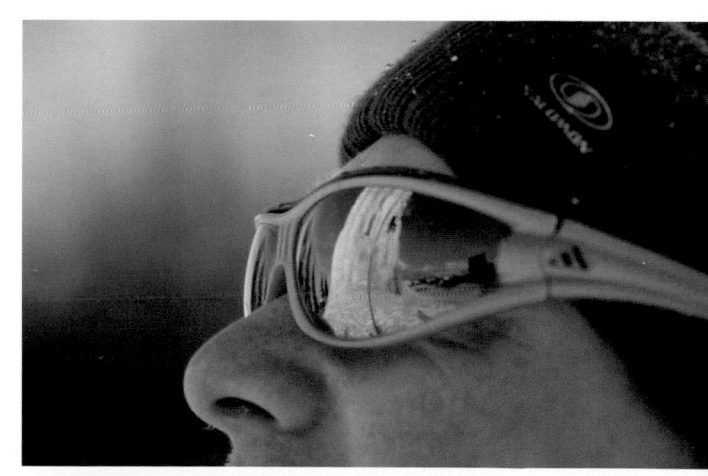

'Surely Britain's Competition Ice Climbing Team carried with it as much expectation of glory as its Bobsled team?'

Will Gadd of Canada for his participation in a drinking game that went badly wrong at the first Pitztal event. Encouraged all the way by ourselves, Will lost his footing whilst hanging upside-down from a beam in the ceiling and attempting to snort a shot of tequila. He came crashing down on the bar, breaking it clean in two and causing us all to be evicted. It was a far cry from the intensity that had put us off the indoor rock competitions years ago.

It was always great to be the underdogs – surely Britain's Competition Ice Climbing Team carried with it as much expectation of glory as its Bobsled team? But it was a chance to meet some inspiring characters and pick up some healthy tricks for the tool box. After all, it's not often you figure-of-4 your way across an ice roof and then hang from a heel spur to rest when you're gully bashing on Ben Nevis. It's all climbing at the end of the day.

Daniel Dulac warms up in Quebec 02 NG
Tim in the qualifier, Quebec 02 IP
Tim warming up, Kirov 02 TE coll
Tim signs his first and last
autograph, Kirov 02 TE coll

RUSSIA

Moscow skyline TE
Daniel Dulac in the
semis at Kirov 02 TE
Daniel Dulac sticks the dyno
in the finals at Kirov 02 TE
Kirov tower TE
Kirov crowd TE

Kirov, Russia
Tim

'The crowd of 10,000 was the largest and loudest of any of the ice competitions.'

The scene was set. The imminent 5th round of the IWC to be held in Kirov, Russia was drawing closer. I was ranked 3rd overall and all I had to do was make it out there to have a strong chance of getting on the podium. I was totally mad for it. But as I checked in at the airport, the draconian airport supervisor informed me that I would not be travelling as I didn't have a visa. I had been let down by my travel agent and felt the whole thing slip away, but I wasn't giving up without a struggle. The next 24 hours were spent on a frantic whirlwind chase around the UK in an attempt to get a visa in time for the comp. I finally made it to the Russian Embassy in London, with my flight re-scheduled to the last possible slot and with crucial seconds to spare, only to be told that it wasn't going to happen because of a trivial detail concerning my invitation. All the tension that had built up seemed to dissipate through my feet into the floor. I was dazed, confused and totally gutted.

But a year later, I settled the score. I got my visa without incident and made it out to Kirov for a truly unforgettable experience. The crowd of 10,000 was the largest and loudest of any of the ice competitions. Added to that, Kirov had been at the centre of a major arms manufacturing unit, so Europeans had been banned from going there until very recently. The Russians were so inquisitive and children would go off in search of their English-speaking friends in order to ask me questions. Even the train journey back, AKA 'The Super Final', was a memorable occasion, and a life-sized glass shotgun filled with local vodka was the prize for anyone who was still hungry for a further taste of success.

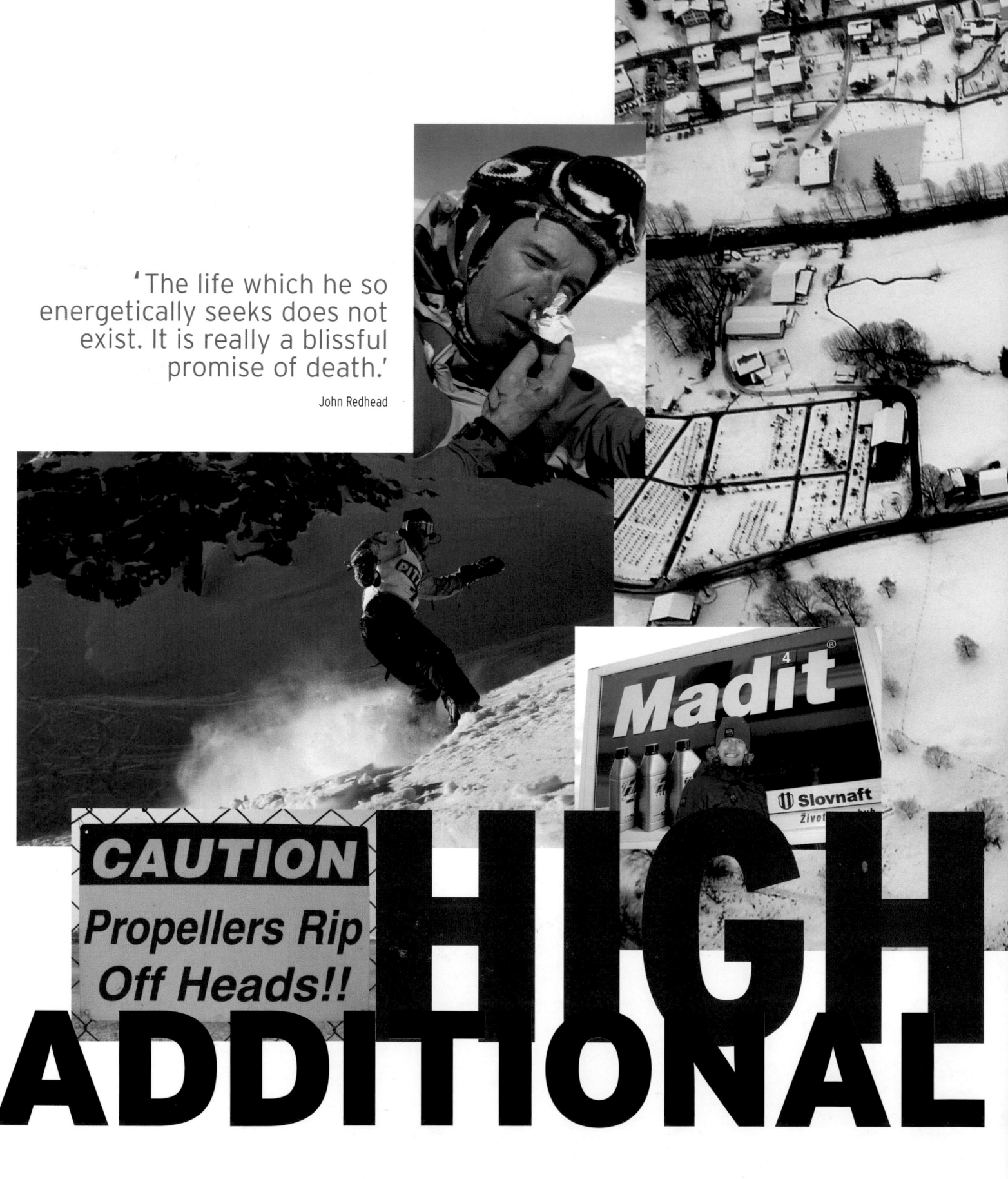

'The life which he so energetically seeks does not exist. It is really a blissful promise of death.'

John Redhead

CAUTION
Propellers Rip
Off Heads!!

ADDITIONAL HIGH

JINX STIMULATION

Mark Garthwaite's nose job in Val D'isère! NG
Neil rides the Valé Blanche, Chamonix TE
'Madit!' TE coll
'Propellers' TE coll
Tim BASE jumps Stauback Falls (900 ft)
Lauterbrunan, Switzerland MF
Slackline feet JK
Tim snow leaping IP

SNOW BOARD

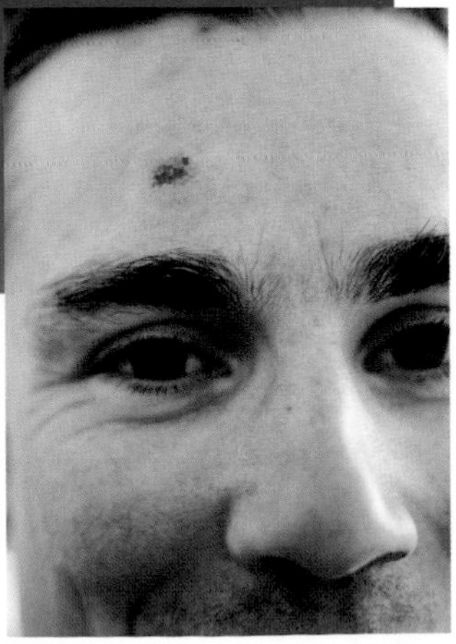

Leo Houlding rides back country
at Alpe d'Huez, France TE
Tignes back country NG
Tim takes air in Alpe d'Huez PT
Neil after ice head-but IP

Highline at Black Rocks
JK

It was Leo Houlding and Patch Hammond who first extolled the virtues of slacklining to us after their infamous trip to Yosemite in 1998. The locals in Camp 4 showed them how to tension a length of climbing tape between two trees and they were completely hooked by the time they left for Thailand on the final leg of their journey. On arrival at Railay Bay, they promptly rejected the local sport climbing in favour of full moon parties followed by extended day time practice sessions to hone their skills on the line. It takes a while to figure it out, but when it finally clicks, slacklining almost feels like walking on air. Add some height to the equation and you're practically there.

HIGHLINE

Nicky's Leap, 80 ft, Vivian Quarry, North Wales
Neil NG coll

The jump that is much sort after (by idiots), Nicky's Leap is a straight 80 foot jump into 80 feet of still water. It is well worth throwing a stone off first in order to break the surface tension and also to wear a stout pair of shoes. I did neither of these things because I was young and foolish, and spent the rest of the week feeling like I'd been walking on hot coals. Not recommended.

NICKY'S LEAP

BASE

BASE

I have always thought that the most memorable experiences are the ones that take you closest to the red line. Whether topping out on a bold grit route, or reaching base camp, delirious and emaciated after conquering a mountain, it is these situations that remain everlasting in your thoughts. Standing at an exit point with a parachute strapped to your back, preparing to jump into space, gives a moment of clarity that feels more real than any I have ever known. You can stay there all day in total safety, have a picnic with your family if you fancy, but as soon as you leave your perch, you will be hurtling towards the ground like a formula one motorbike accelerating towards a large building. Bang, the parachute opens, and with careful positioning, you land safely. It sounds insane, but just like with climbing, the more you learn about your game, the more you reduce the risk. And then there's the future potential to merge BASE skills with deep water soloing tactics on huge cliffs. You would need to refine your exit strategy so you could cut loose with the grace and eloquence of a cliff diver. But a combination of these disciplines could be the catalyst for a new level, hybrid extreme sport. Imagine free soloing a big wall with a parachute, on-sight, at your limit. No queues there then!

Leo Houlding hangs out RG
Tims wingsuit madness! TE coll
Tim BASE jumps Cheddar Gorge (330 ft) TE coll/PT
Tim & Leo after the first of many GF

'If you slip into a rigid comfort zone then you are dying – slowly, but still dying.'

Arno Ilgner

Editor:

Neil Gresham

Art director and production manager:

Sam Grimmer

Principle photography:

Mike Robertson

Ian Parnell

Ray Wood

Additional photography:

Neil Gresham
Tim Emmett
Grant Farquhar
Mark Garthwaite
Mike Goldwater
Seb Grieve
Andi Heckenberger
Andy Parkin
Cameron Lawson
Dave Pegler
Charles Pertwee
Paul Twomey
Jules Kelly
Paul Twomey
Raoul Gravell
Mike Francis

Neil and Tim would like to thank:

Louise Gresham, Ken Wilson, Charlie Woodburn, Mark Garthwaite, Seb Grieve, Grant Farquhar, Rick Smee, Matt 'Smythe' Smith, Del Smith, Leo Houlding, Andy Cave, Nick Dixon, Leah Crane, Mark Campbell, Patch Hammond, Martin Atkinson, Adam Wainwright, Ken Palmer, Klem Loskott, Gav Symmonds, Jules Kelly, Steve Bunting, Steve Pack, Steve Lawler, Kelvin Briscall, Rich 'Dallas' Collins, Andy Coish, Dave Pegler, Sandy Ogilvie, Adrian Berry, Alan Kerr, Fabiano Ferrera, Miguel Riera, Ting, Tang & Tong, Gal, Abel Fleitas Cruz, Corry Taylor, Pete Rostron, Christian Jaeggi, Thomas Hodel, Paul Cornthwaite, Frank Bennett, Lorenzo Delladio, Oscar Durbiano, Fabrizio Vesco, Damian Cook, Jules Cartwright, Paul Innes, Andy Clarke, Chris Williams, Geoff Pearson, Chris Henshall, Shaun Ellison, Grant Wright, Nick Singleton, Jon Wilson, Mike Weeks, Bean Sopwith, Paul Pritchard, George Smith, Simon Kincaid, Gerry Smith.

Sam would like to thank:

Christy McCarthy, Stephen Ungar, Stephen White, Louise Coulthard, Darren Mcintosh, Deidre White, Fraser Crozier, Paul Aikman and Michael Badham, without whose support, assistance, patience and advice, this project would never have come to fruition.

'To refuse to be cast down, that is the lesson. Walk on and see a new view. Walk on and see birds fly. Walk on and leave behind all things that dam up the inlet of experience.'

Bruce Lee